L Y N N   S T E R N

U N V E I L I N G S

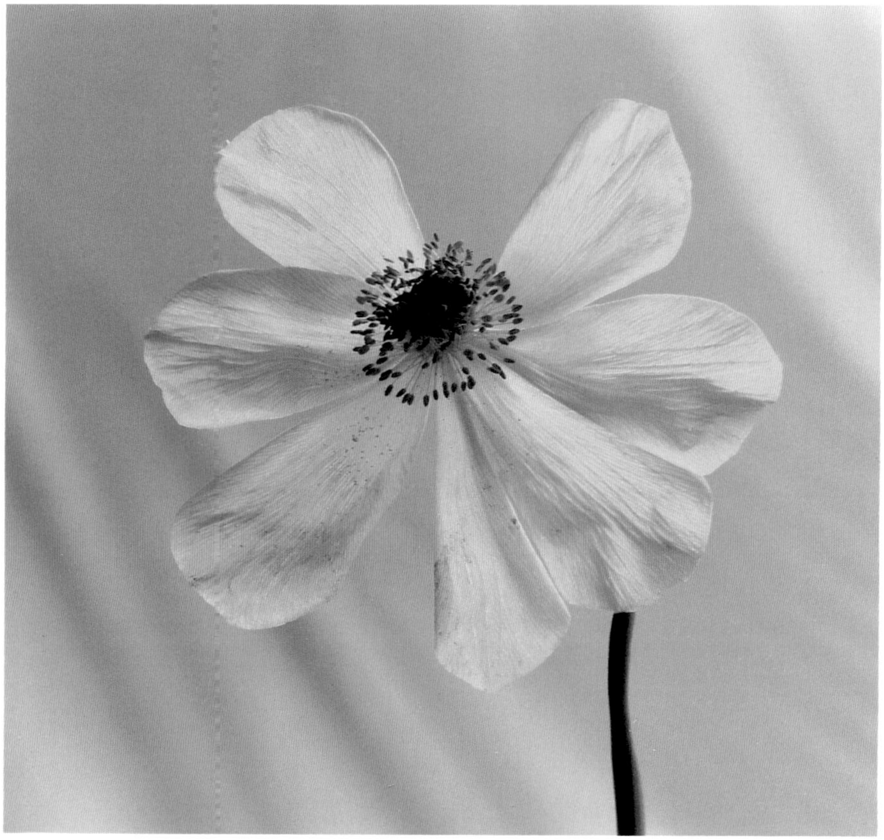

LYNN STERN

UNVEILINGS

FOREWORD BY

PAUL CAPONIGRO

ESSAY BY

DIANE WAKOSKI

HUDSON HILLS PRESS • NEW YORK

Library of Congress Catalog Number 88-90781
ISBN 1-55595-020-5

First edition

Published in the United States by Hudson Hills Press, Inc.,
Suite 1308, 230 Fifth Avenue, New York, NY 10001-7704.

Editor and Publisher: Paul Anbinder

Distributed in the United States, its territories and possessions, Canada, Mexico, and Central and South America
by Rizzoli International Publications, Inc.
Distributed in the United Kingdom, Eire, Europe, Israel, and the Middle East by Phaidon Press Limited.
Distributed in Australia by Bookwise International.
Distributed in Japan by Yohan (Western Publications Distribution Agency).
Distributed in South Korea by Nippon Shuppan Hanbai.

ACKNOWLEDGMENTS

Unveilings would not have come to fruition without the help of my husband, Jeremy Lang. I relied heavily on his discerning eye, his constant support, and his remarkable willingness to continue offering criticisms despite their frequently poor reception.

I am very grateful to Paul Caponigro for his faith in *Unveilings*—and for much else. Although I have never formally studied with him, I have benefitted enormously from assisting him in the darkroom; his reviews of my work have been invaluable learning experiences. Paul has listened as well as looked, and has always understood my desire to photograph what isn't there.

Many people viewed *Unveilings* as a book mock-up and contributed to it through their suggestions and encouragement. I am indebted to all of them. In particular, I would like to thank Charles Chetham, Director of the Smith College Museum of Art, who proposed an exhibition of these photographs at the museum, and whose sensitivity and enthusiasm made working on the show a pleasure.

My thanks go to F. W. Battenfeld & Son in Red Hook, New York, who grew the exquisite hybrid anemones I photographed. Fred Battenfeld and Clifford Platt were especially helpful in taking me through the greenhouses on several occasions so I could select particular flowers.

FOR JEREMY

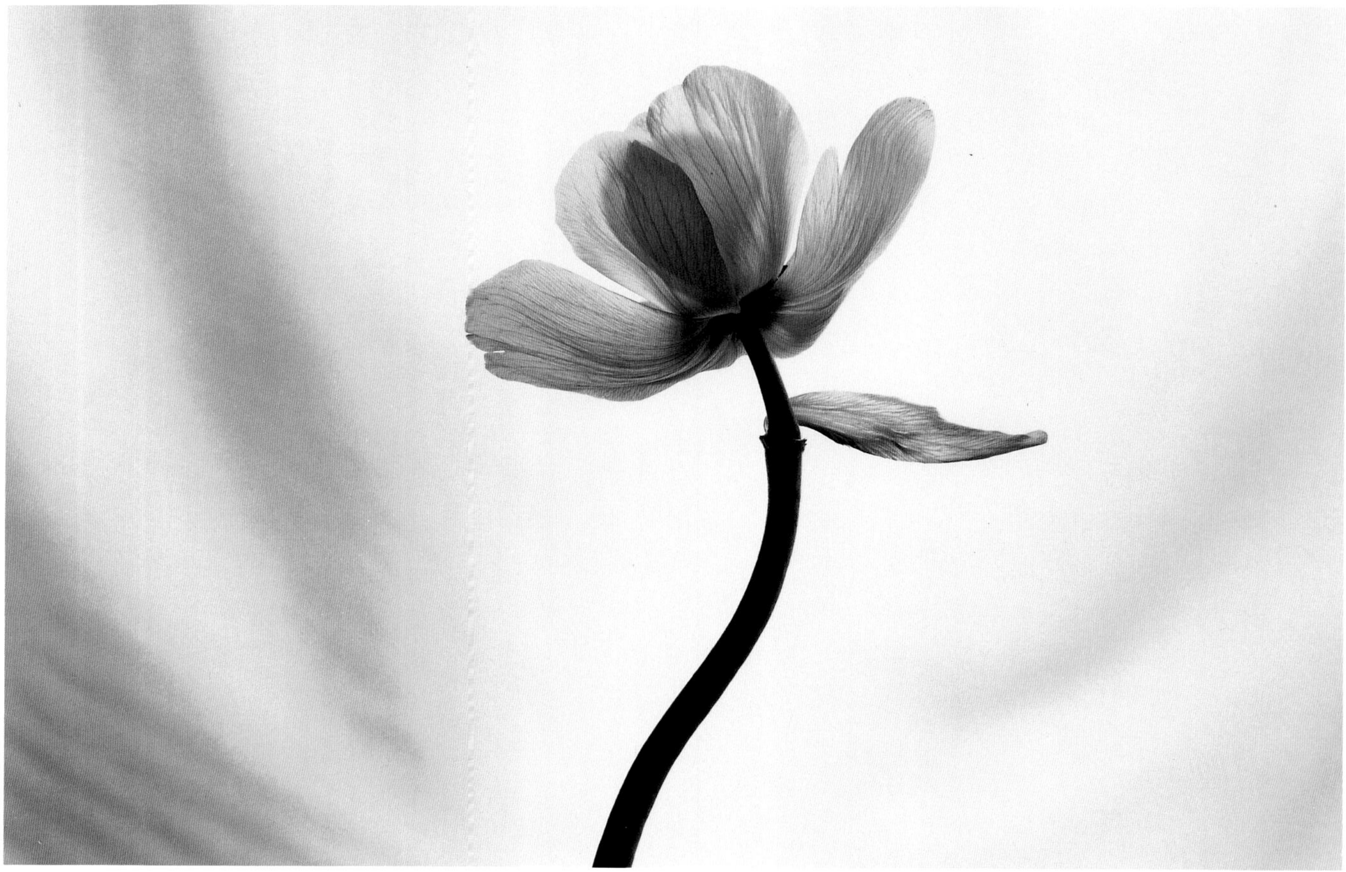

THE BEAUTIFUL CHANGES

One wading a Fall meadow finds on all sides
The Queen Anne's Lace lying like lilies
On water; it glides
So from the walker, it turns
Dry grass to a lake, as the slightest shade of you
Valleys my mind in fabulous blue Lucernes.

The beautiful changes as a forest is changed
By a chameleon's tuning his skin to it;
As a mantis, arranged
On a green leaf, grows
Into it, makes the leaf leafier, and proves
Any greenness is deeper than anyone knows.

Your hands hold roses always in a way that says
They are not only yours; the beautiful changes
In such kind ways,
Wishing ever to sunder
Things and things' selves for a second finding, to lose
For a moment all that it touches back to wonder.

RICHARD WILBUR

AN OFFERING OF THE HEART

In the world of photography today, where intellectual complexity and conceptual art hold sway, it is refreshing to encounter work that speaks simply, directly, and to the heart. Lynn Stern works from her inner promptings and avoids pandering to the ongoing clamor for overwrought or shocking images.

The strength of her photography lies in its immediacy and caring; through her camera, Lynn's awareness and sensitivity gently touch her fellow human beings. I admire her courage to create *Unveilings*, a group of apparently similar images, in a world that calls for more and more excitement and change in both art and life, a world driven by the impulse toward rapid, superficial consumption. Unlike many recent photographs, which seem to have been conceived like sensational headlines, Lynn's images embody her meditative stance and deep humaneness, allowing the viewer's experience to take root. Those who seek more than the hollow stimulation of novelty might benefit from the steady building of her observations—and take part in the nourishment that results.

As contrasted with the more organic methods of the other plastic arts, the seeming mechanicalness of photography makes images appear to come easily, or with little serious effort on the part of the artist. However, technique, whether mastered readily or with difficulty, is always the lesser problem in creating. Whatever the medium and however long it may take to become skilled in its use, it eventually becomes merely a vehicle for manifesting the artist's thoughts and emotions. The artist's real challenge is to make voice and vision transcend the medium; this is what distinguishes truly good work.

To my mind, the photographs in *Unveilings* display a naïveté, an openness, and an almost childlike simplicity. Concerned with the laying bare of feelings (rather than being about flowers *per se*), they are daring for Lynn personally as well as photographically. Because she is intent on *seeing*, vulnerability and feeling are vital parts of her creative activity.

In the opening photographs, the play of light expresses a simultaneous enveloping and separating of space within the field of the image. As the sequence develops, a flower suddenly emerges from this mysterious interaction, suggesting birth. The juxtaposition of dark values with brighter transparent tones creates a fluidity that resembles a gentle dance of objects within the image; fluidity and movement come as naturally as breath, and Lynn maintains these qualities throughout the series.

Taken individually, each photograph seems a portrait carefully built with the beauty of a light unique to the silver print. Sameness of subject does not effect redundancy; instead, each image offers new details to hold the viewer's attention. Both individually and sequentially, they evoke a persistent unfolding through the light, which vibrates between the forms and their enigmatic backgrounds.

In *Unveilings*, I also find a continuity with Lynn's earlier work. Her desert landscapes, for instance, used the horizon line to bisect the frame into equal masses of empty sky and land; yet, rather than mere emptiness, she managed to capture some essential quality of space. Because she experienced space so intensely, she was able to manifest that in her prints.

The jaded, untrained, or unwilling eye might see in those desert landscapes only a cool space of divisions or shapes, but viewers receptive to the language of photography will be able to feel the space pulsing vibrantly. For Lynn sensed a correspondence within herself, and so arrived at recognition through empathy. Such recognition can marry artist and subject, and it seldom fails to yield effective images for those ready to experience and reveal it.

Inclined to communion through her work, Lynn Stern stays ever in touch with that rare realm of emotion in a state of respect and trust. She has yielded to her subjects and has, thereby, been allowed profound access to them. In *Unveilings*, her art reveals the intangible world permeated by the inner heart.

PAUL CAPONIGRO · SANTA FE, 1987

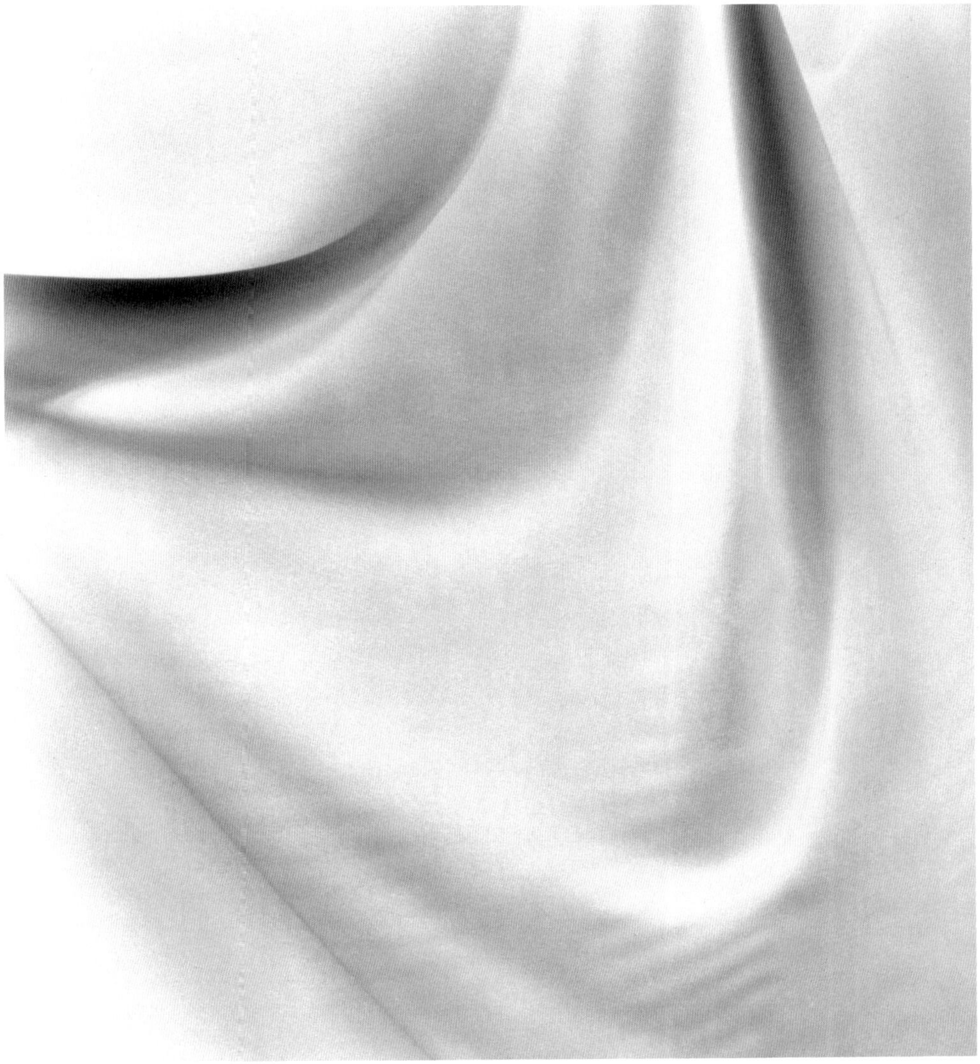

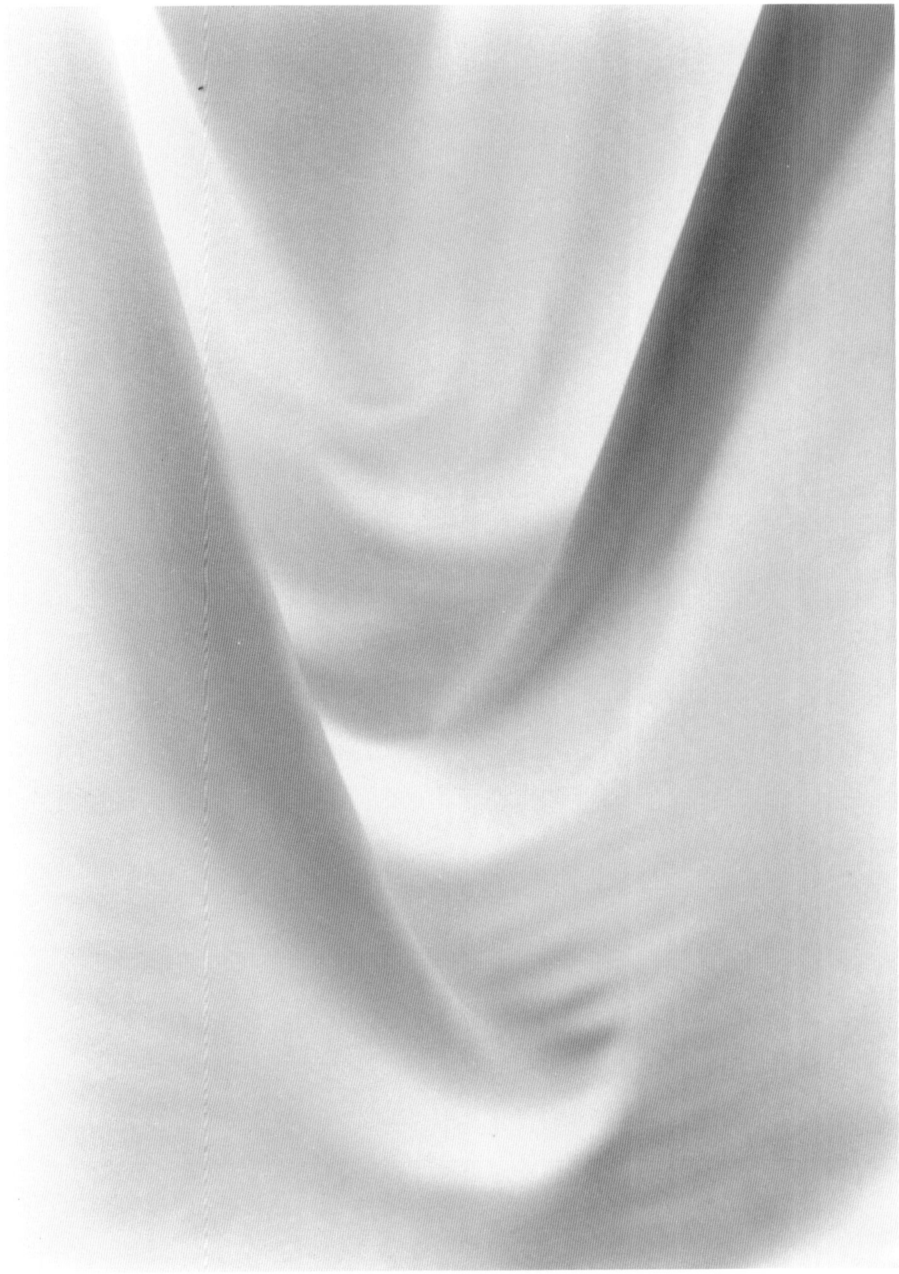

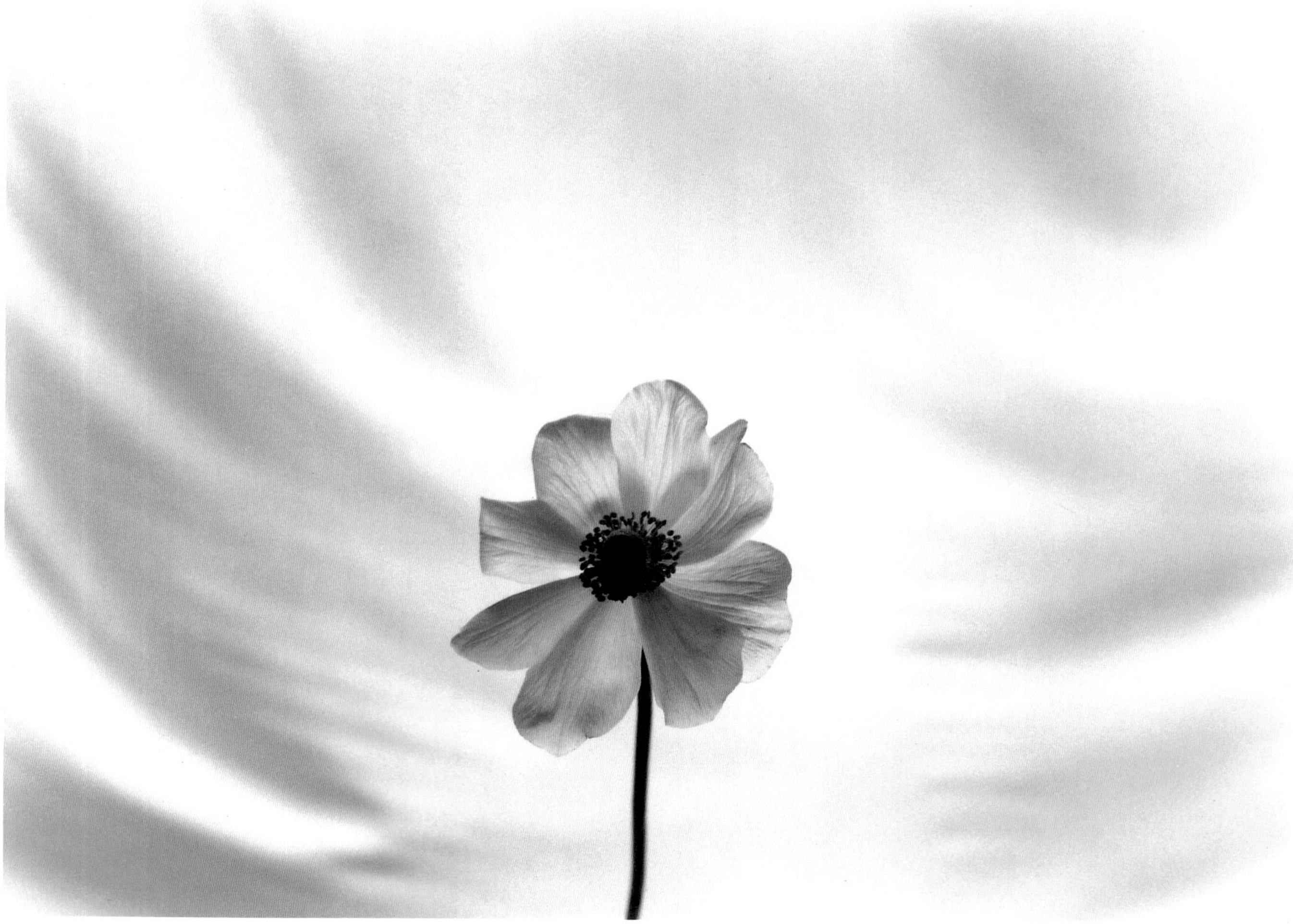

INTRODUCTION

Several years ago, I spent the better part of a winter using a piece of thin satin fabric as a vehicle by which to photograph light. Those efforts were frustrating; graphic and abstract, the elegant forms overwhelmed the mystery of the light. And, ironically, the most successful image pointed to the futility of attempting a series: it seemed complete, incapable of further exploration.

The following photographs resulted from a desire to animate that earlier idea. It occurred to me that if I used two vehicles for the light, their interaction might yield the feeling of energy I sought. And as I proceeded, I did sense an almost palpable vibrancy: a quality of space as much as of light, it seemed to emanate from both the satin and the flowers, yet felt as though it belonged to neither exclusively.

When I began to print the negatives, I became aware of a puzzling but consistent reaction: certain photographs that had both luminosity and movement still felt wanting. As I continued to edit, I realized that what these rejected images lacked was a feeling of depth, not just formally but emotionally as well.

Without having been anthropomorphized, the anemones had become as revealing as human portraits. And, just as a series of portraits has structure, so these images seemed to fall into natural groups based on a certain formal organization: the turned backs; the tentative confrontations; the close-up heads; the full frontalities. Although similarity of stance formed the basis for each of these divisions, it did not preclude overlapping and ambiguity, for "stance" has many connotations. The slight shifts from one section to another were variations on the theme of exposure; throughout, there was a sense of witnessing gestures as evocative as a person's body language. The subtly changing relationships between satin and flowers had created an environment, not only of luminous energy but of poignant emotions: bewilderment, yearning, boldness, frailty.

What began as dialogues in light had become metaphors for vulnerability.

LYNN STERN · NEW YORK, 1987

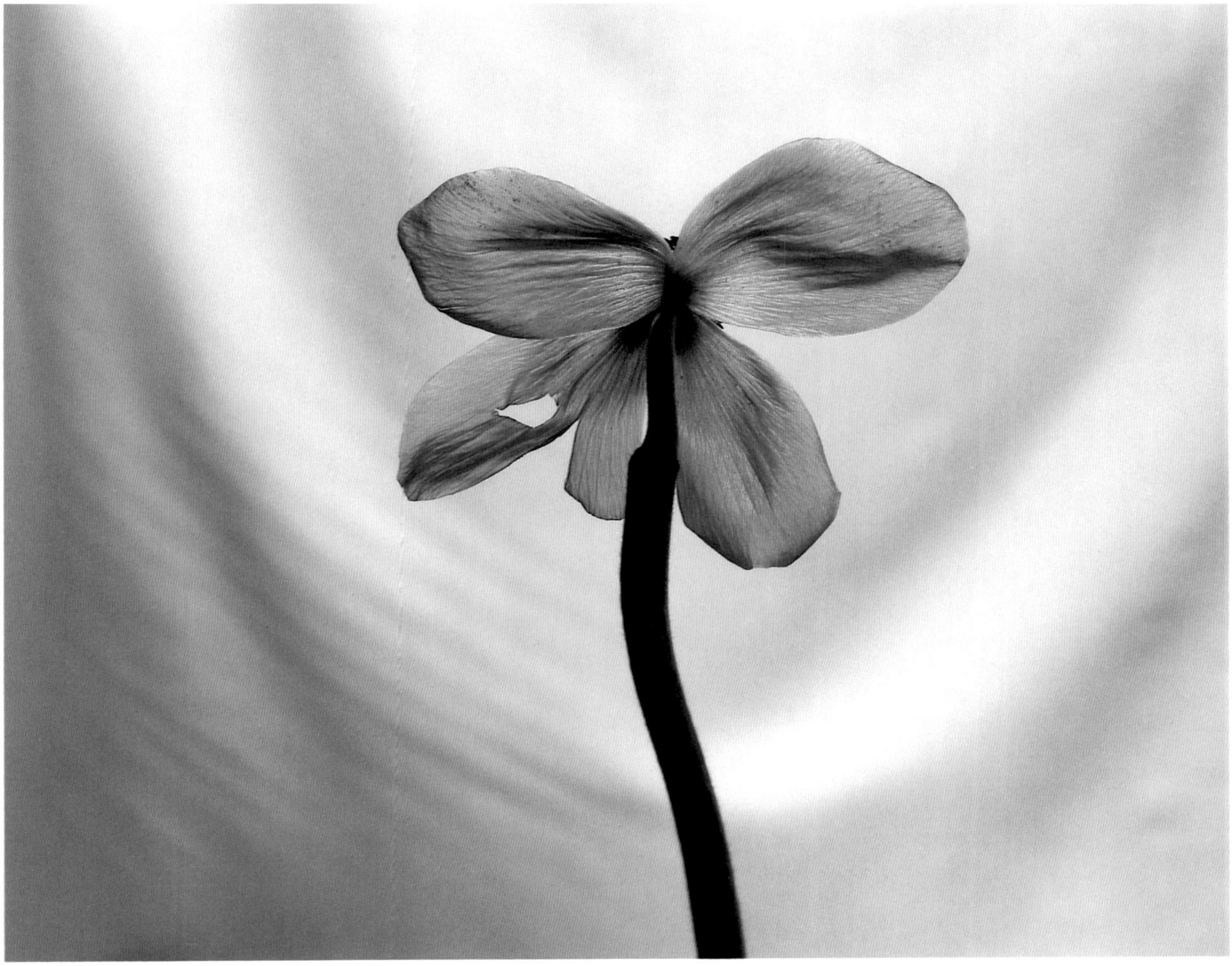

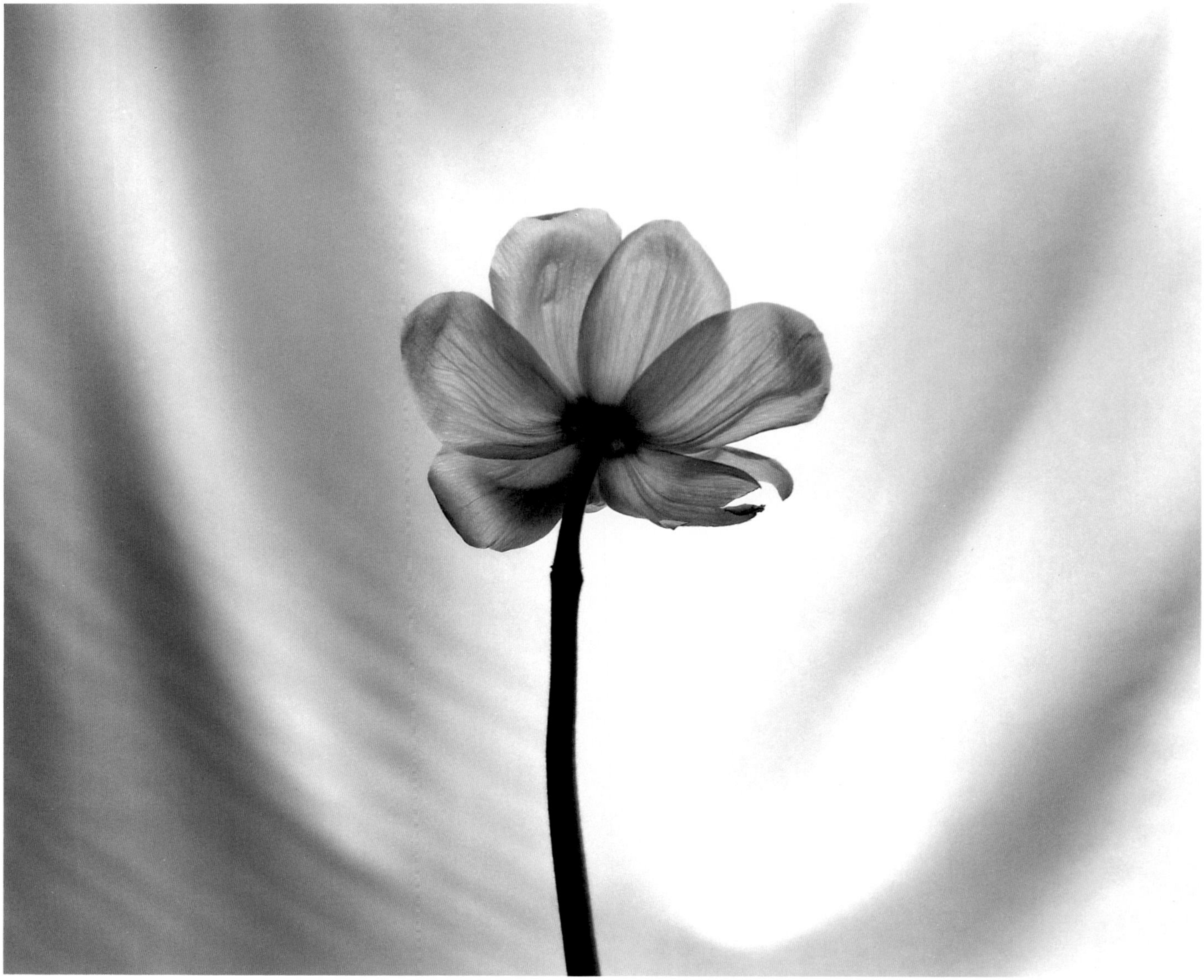

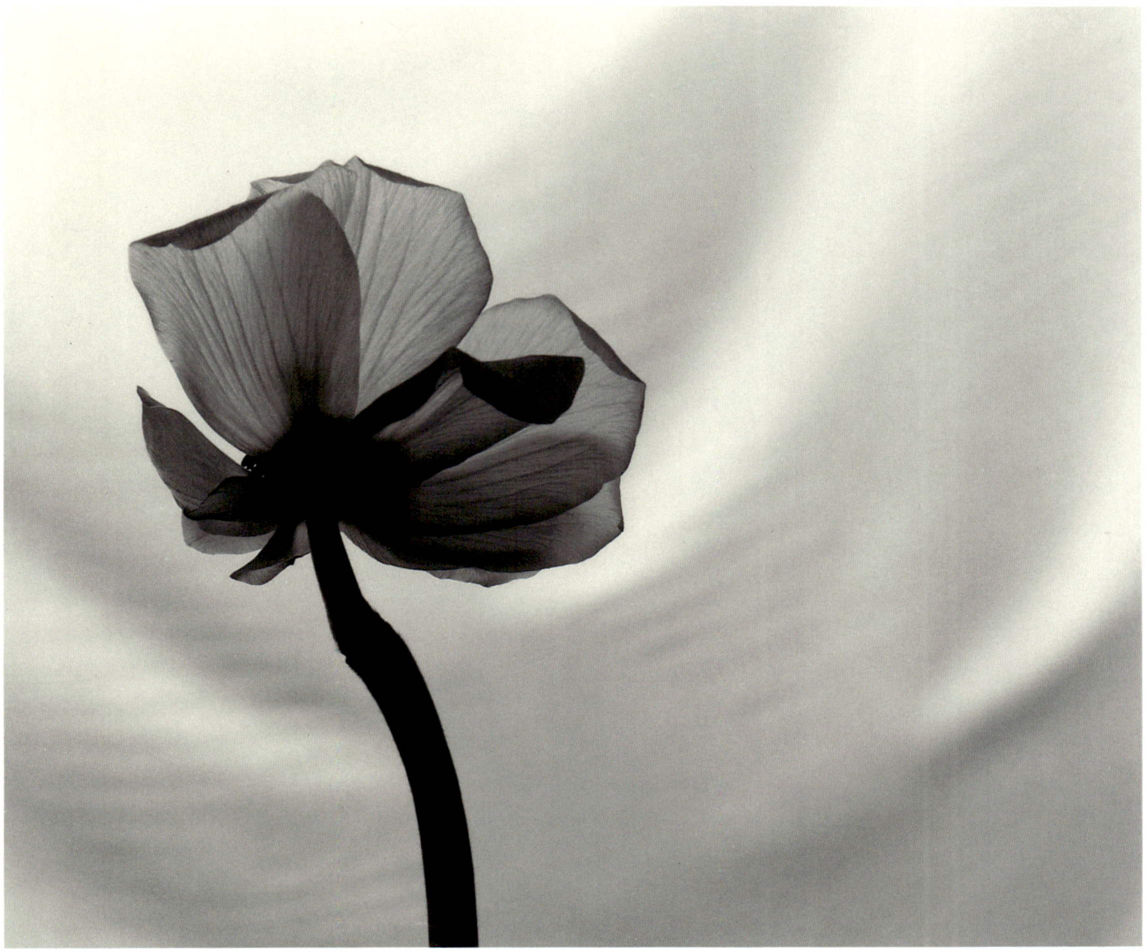

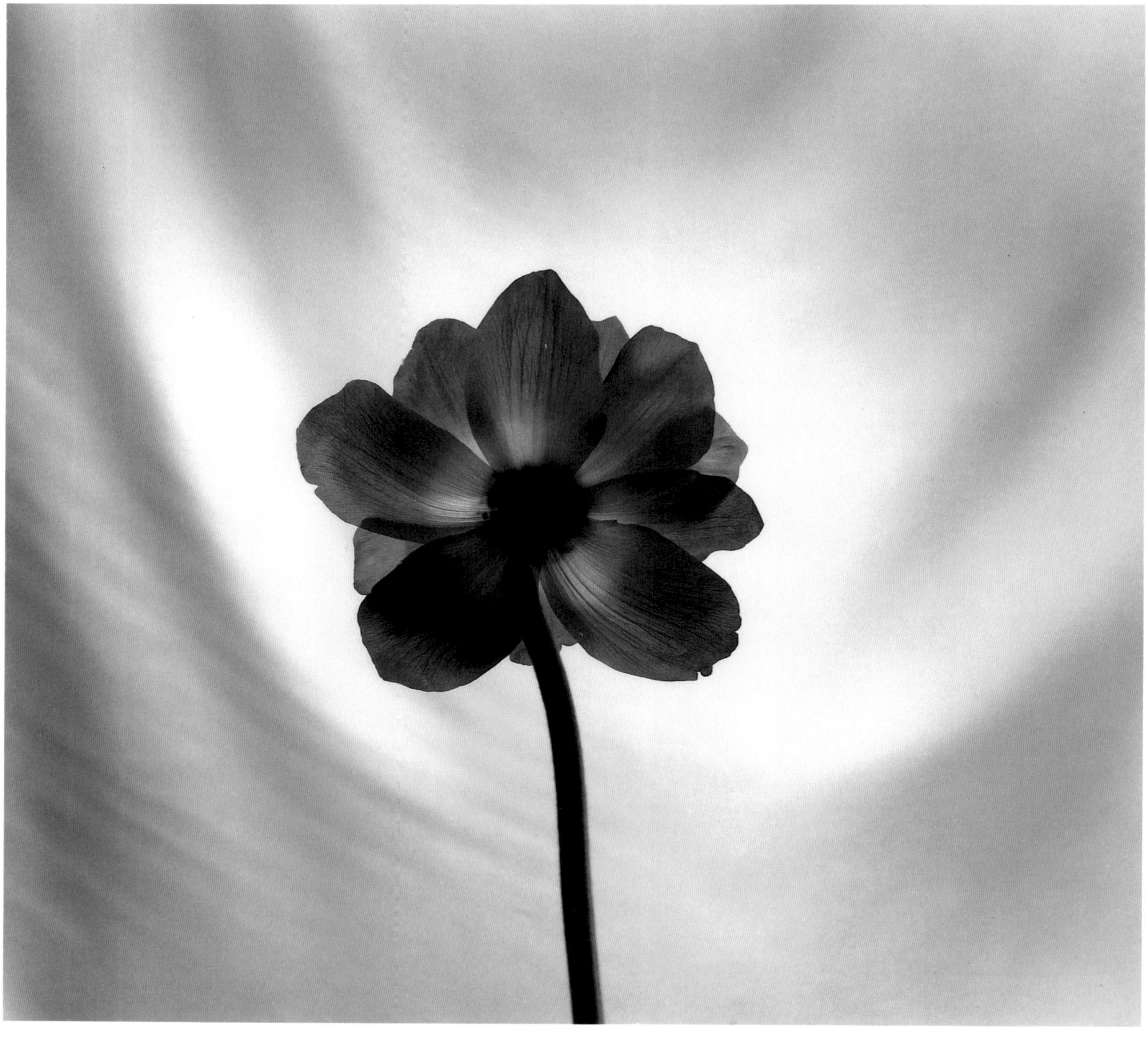

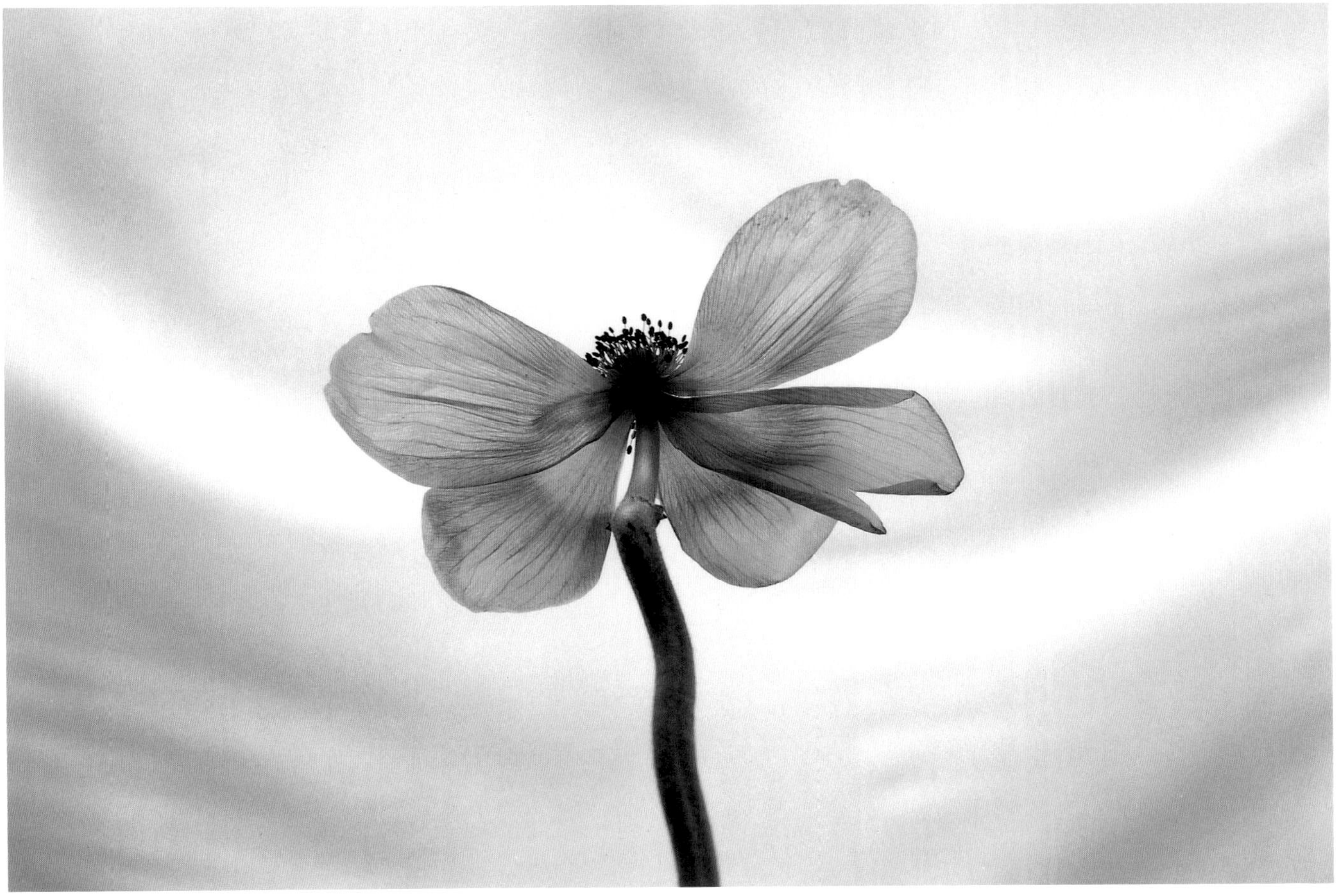

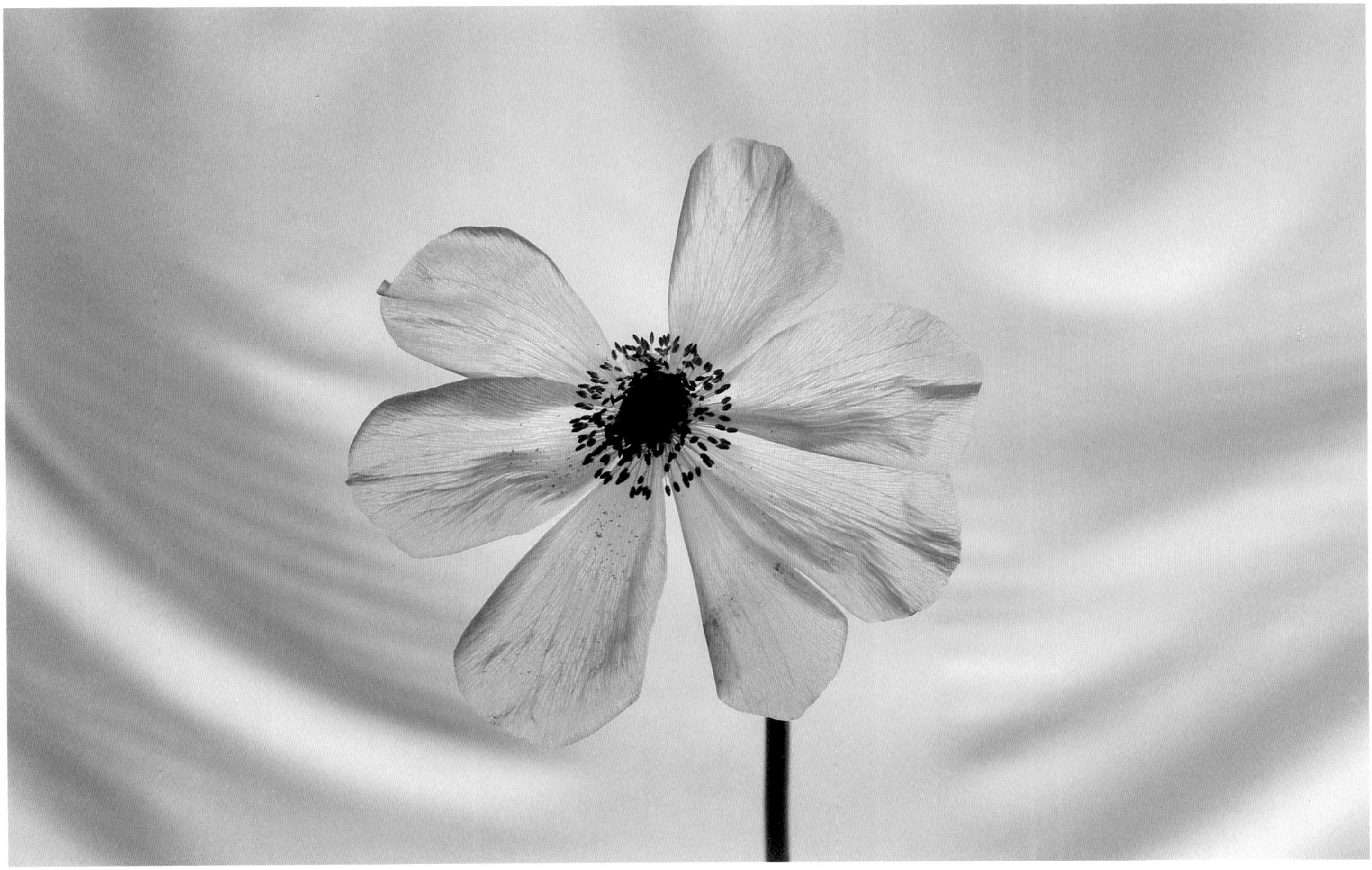

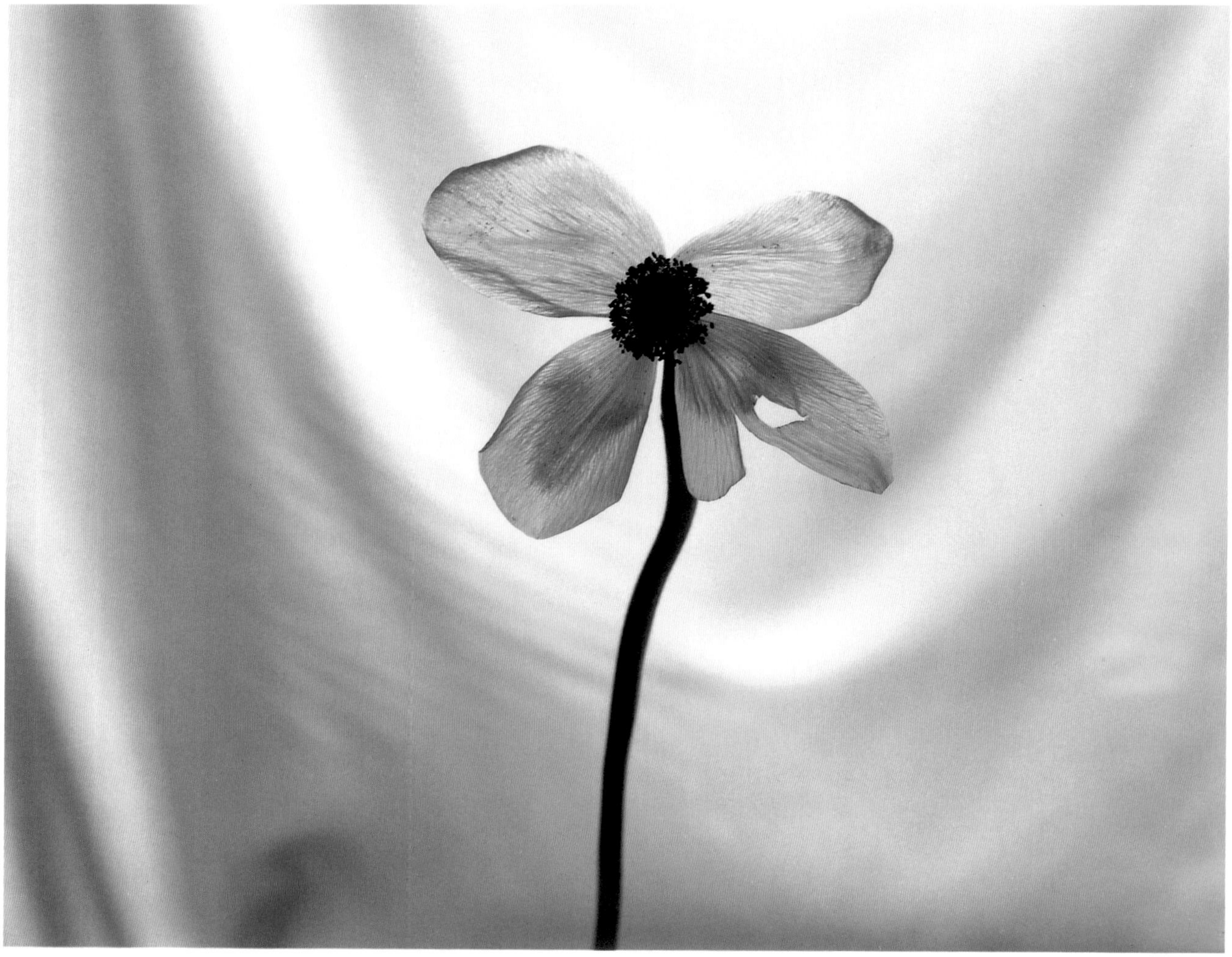

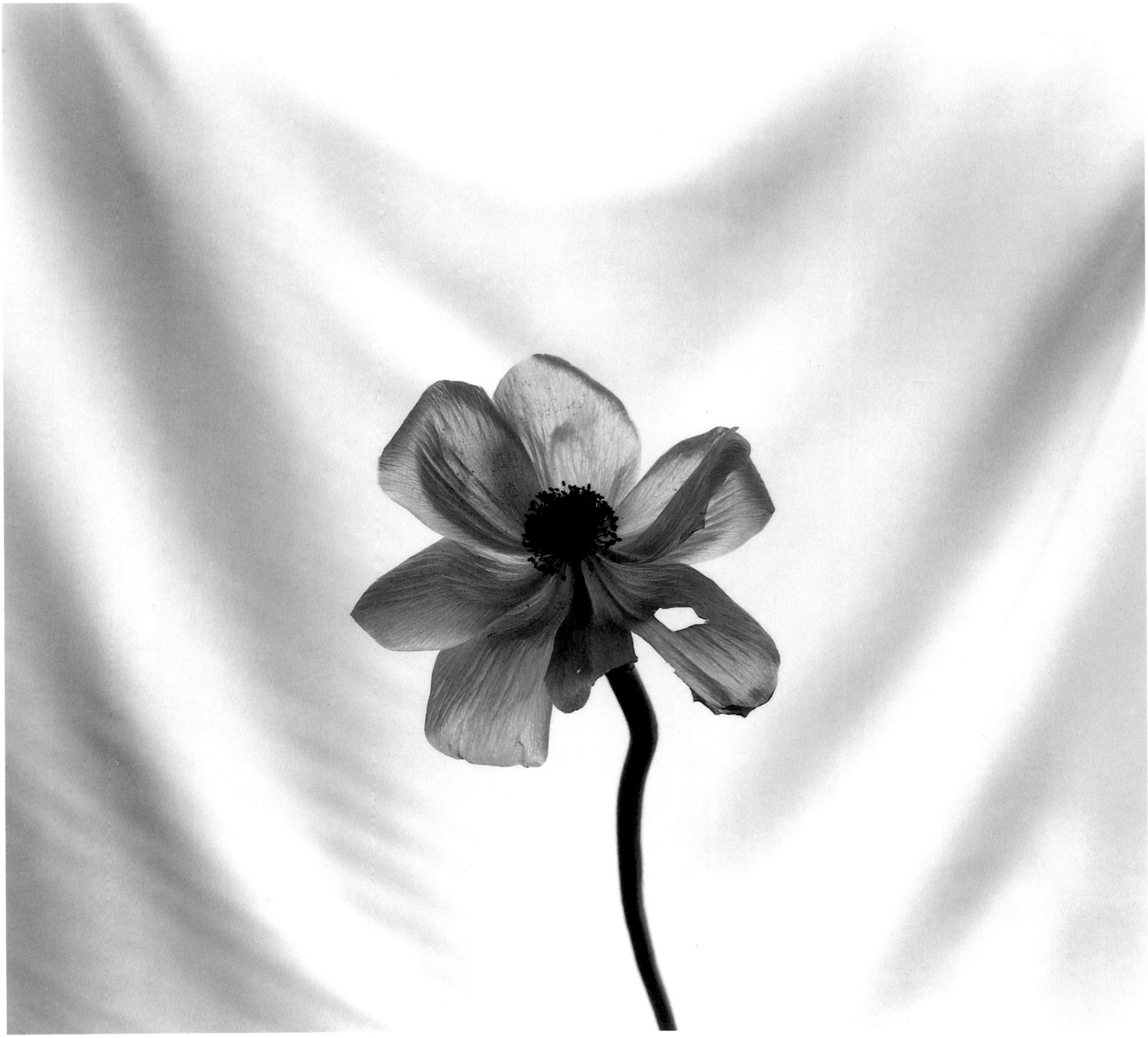

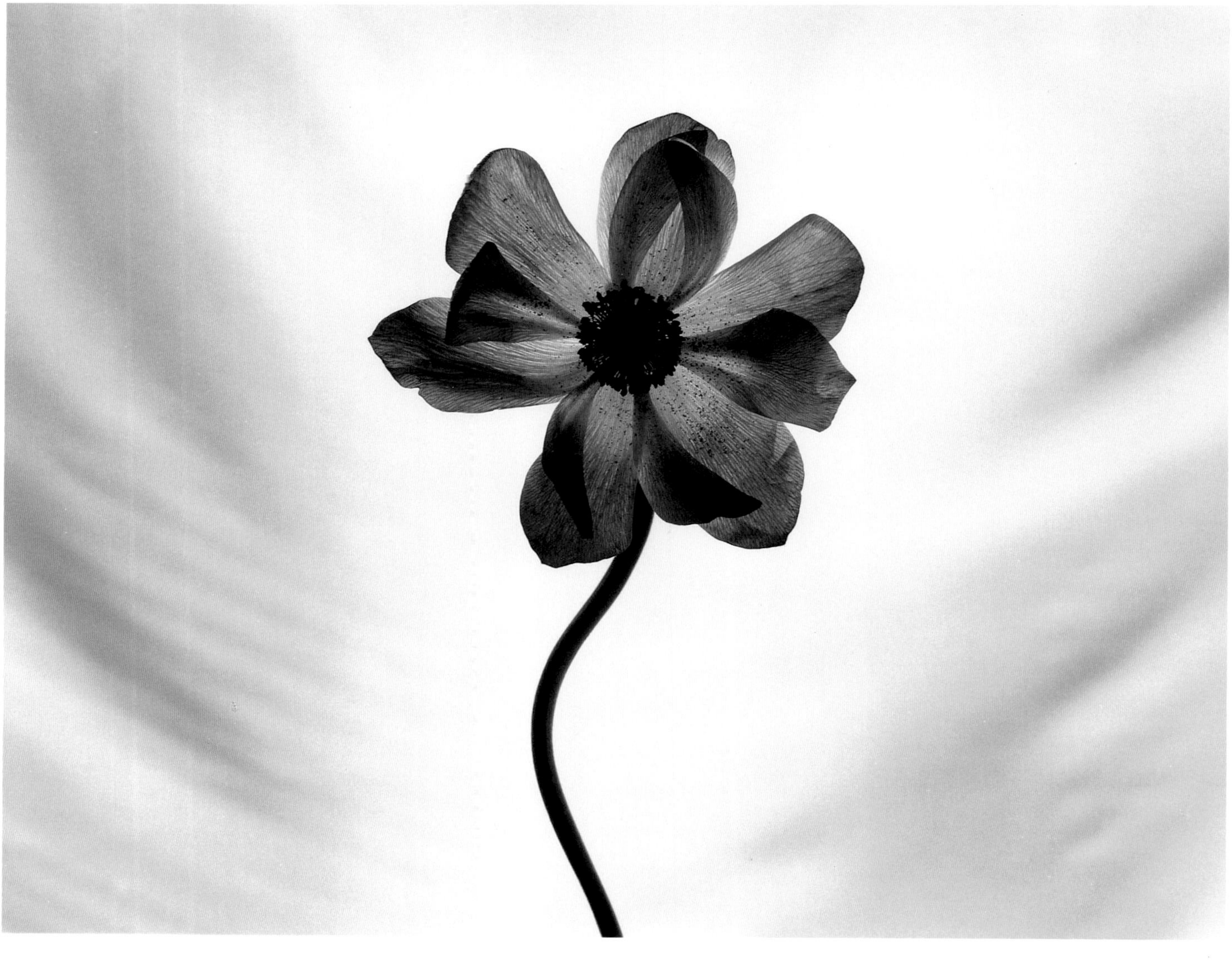

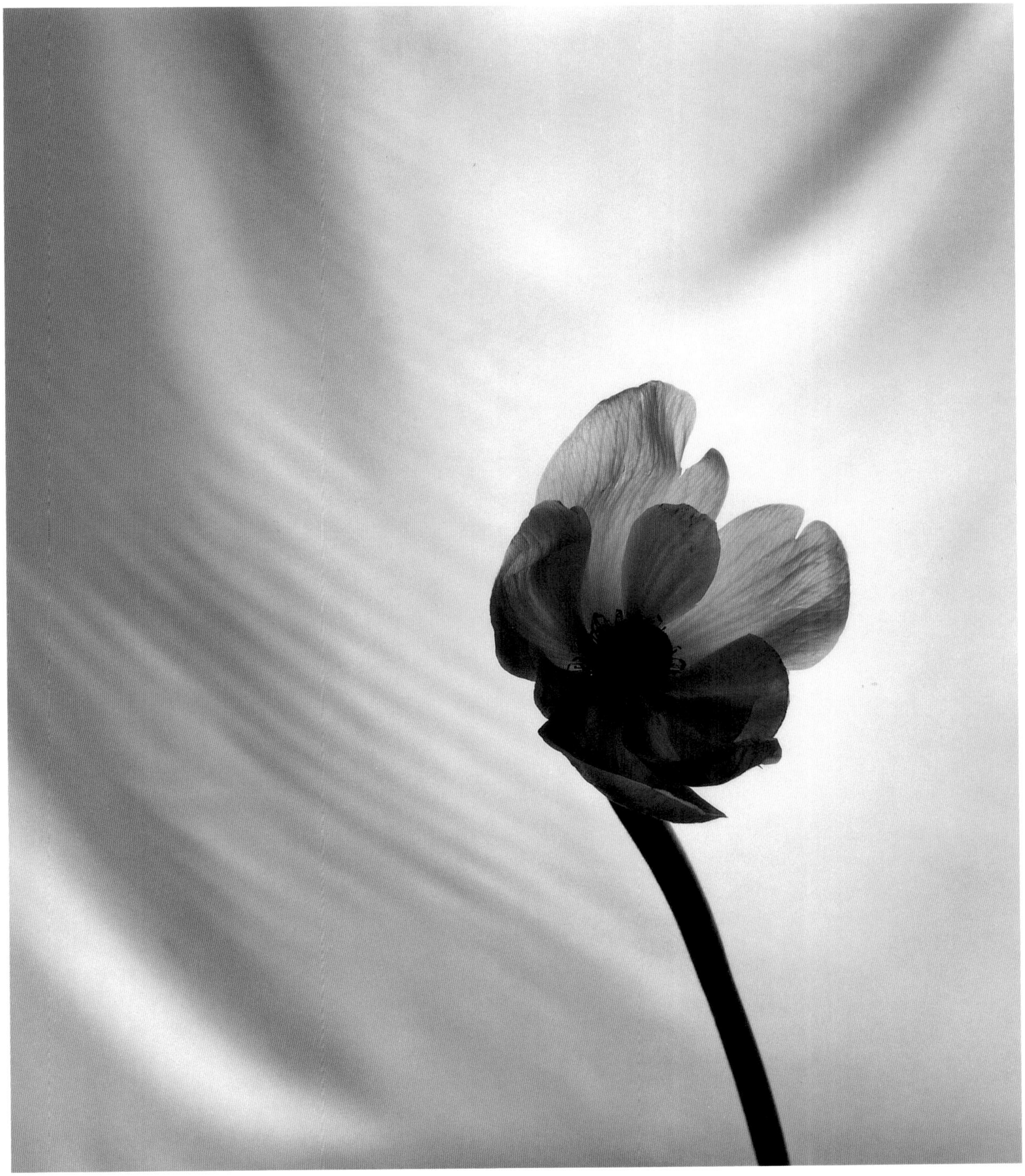

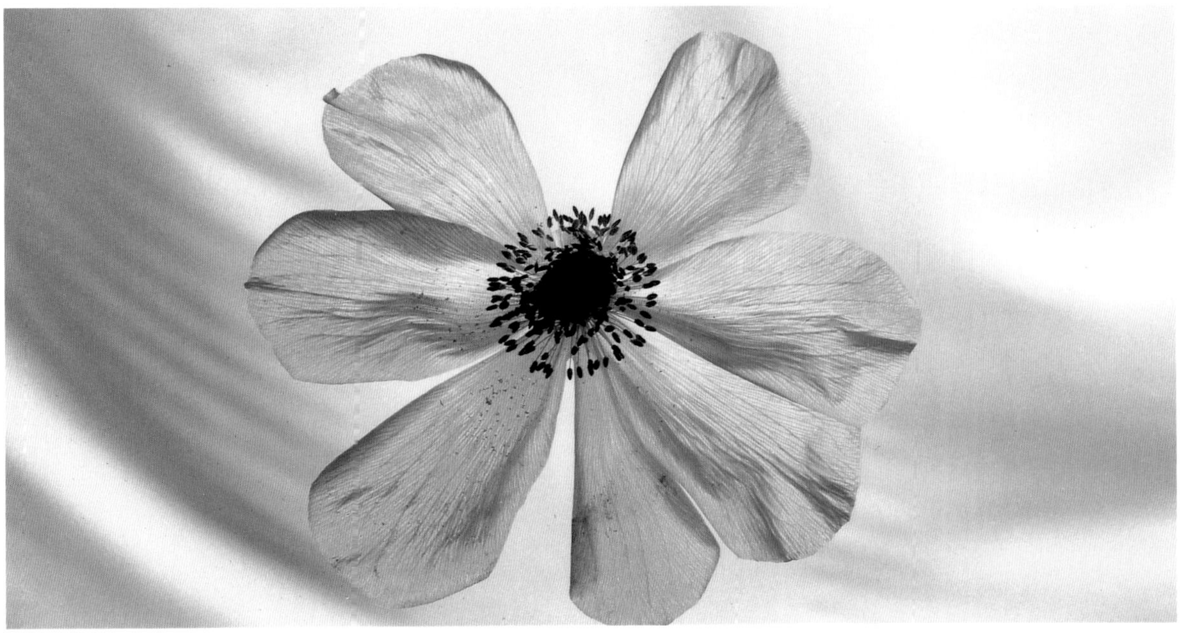

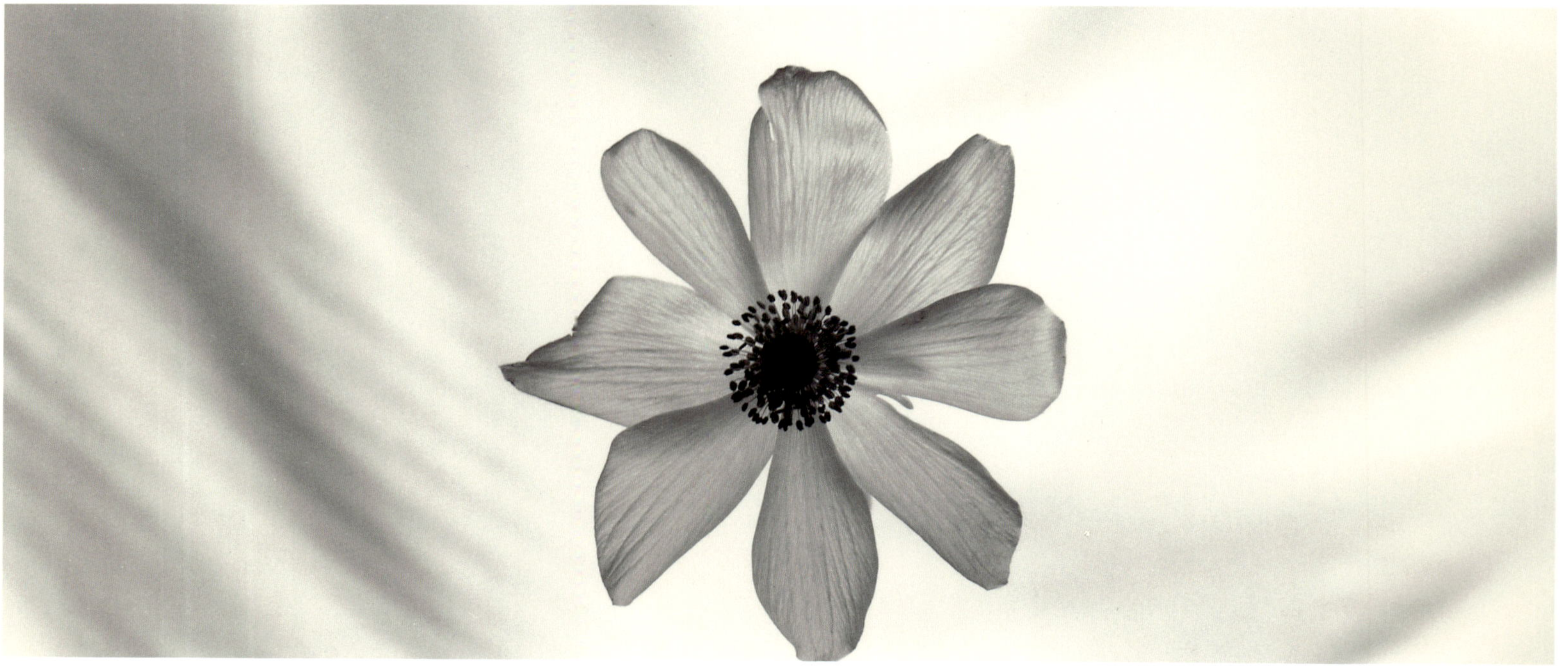

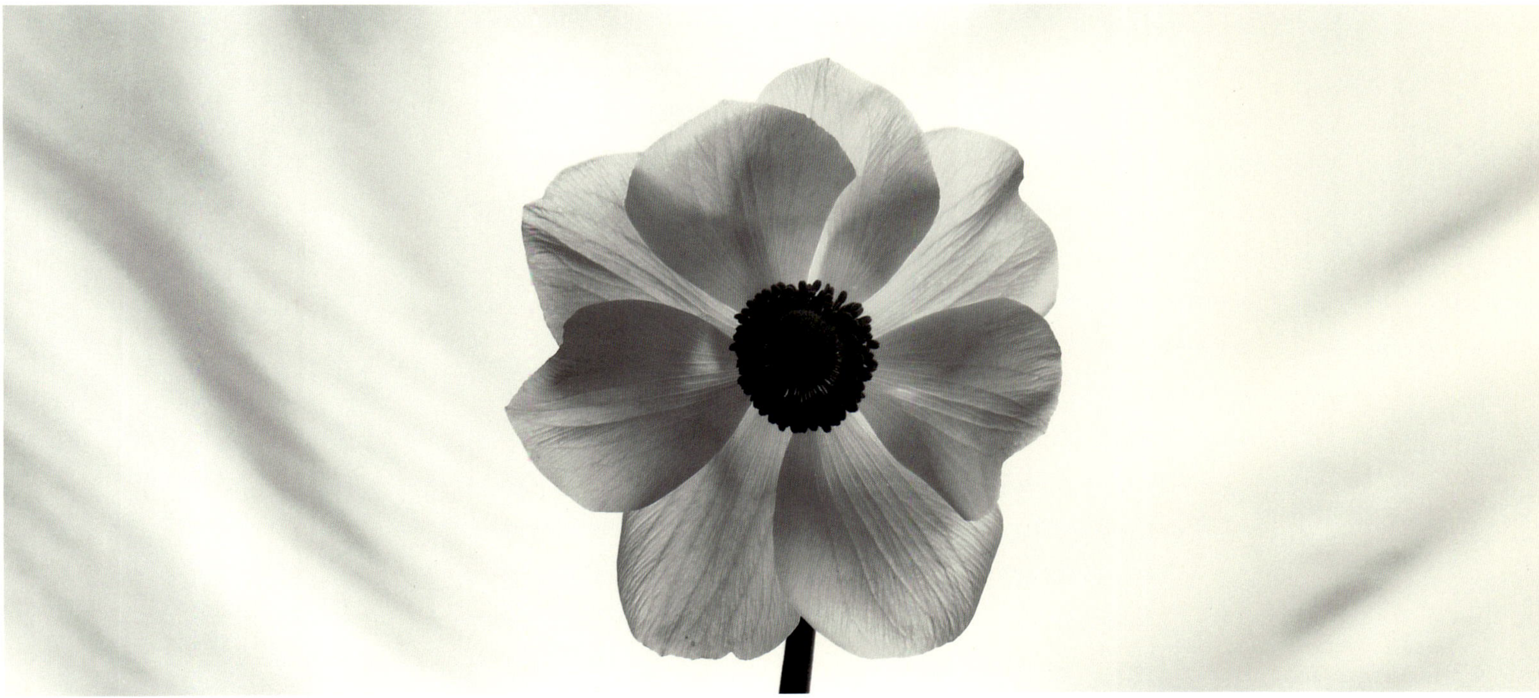

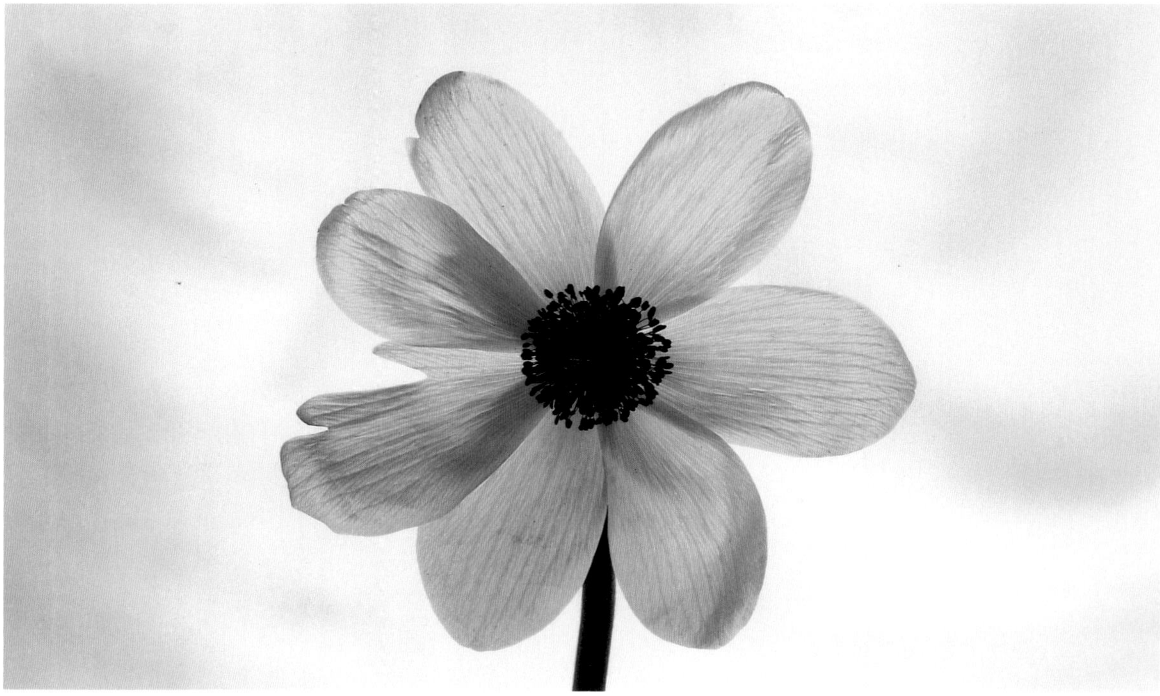

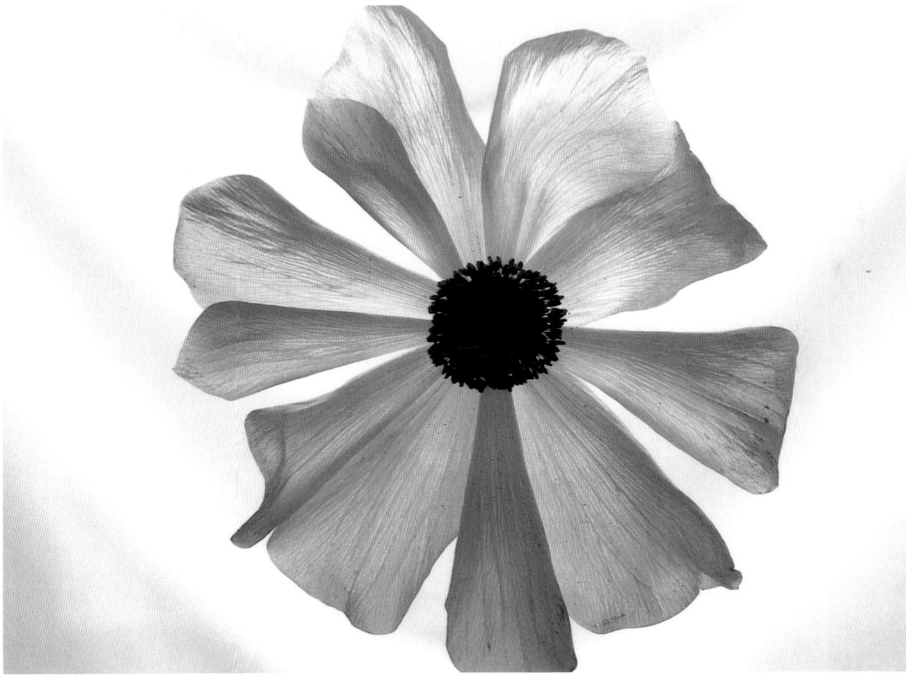

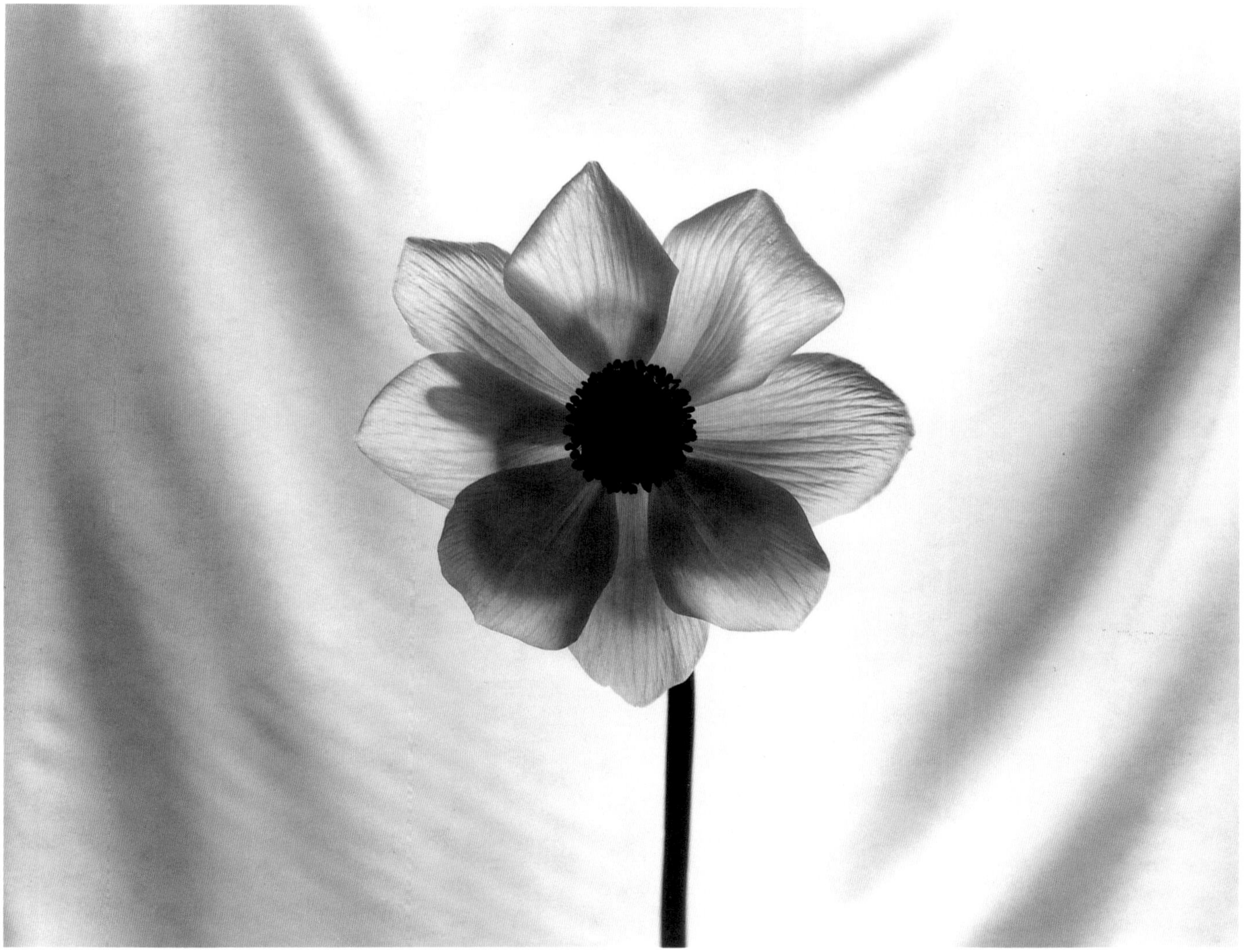

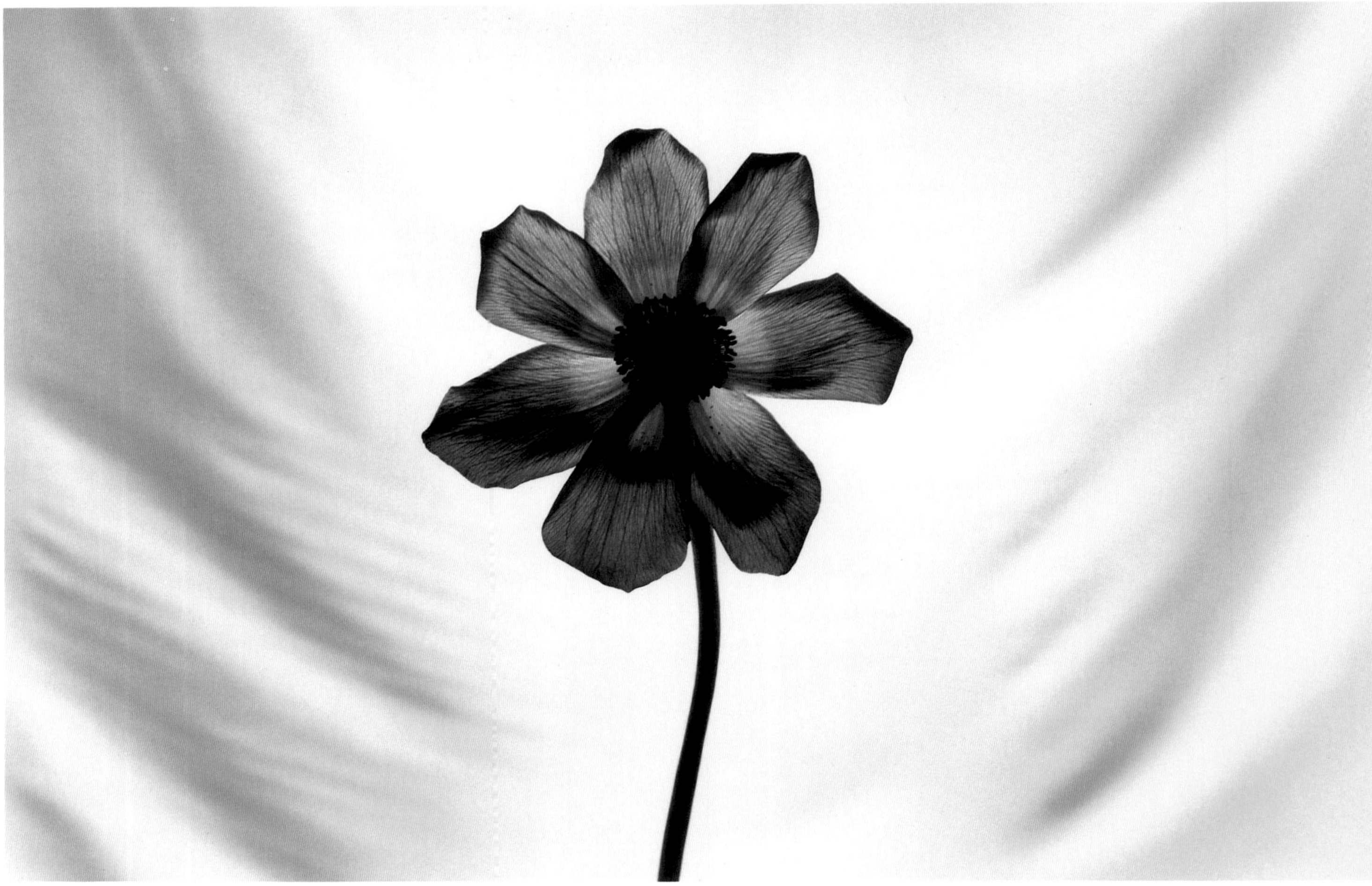

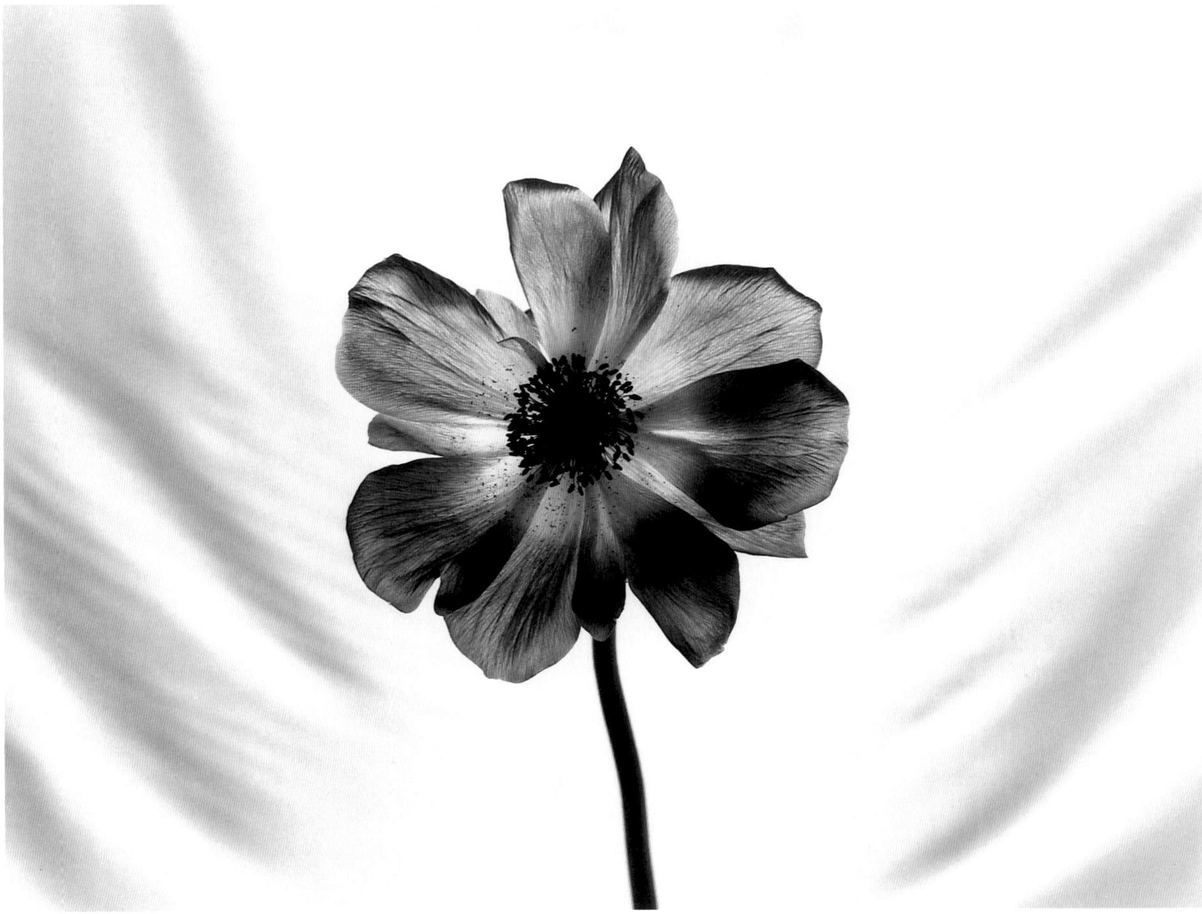

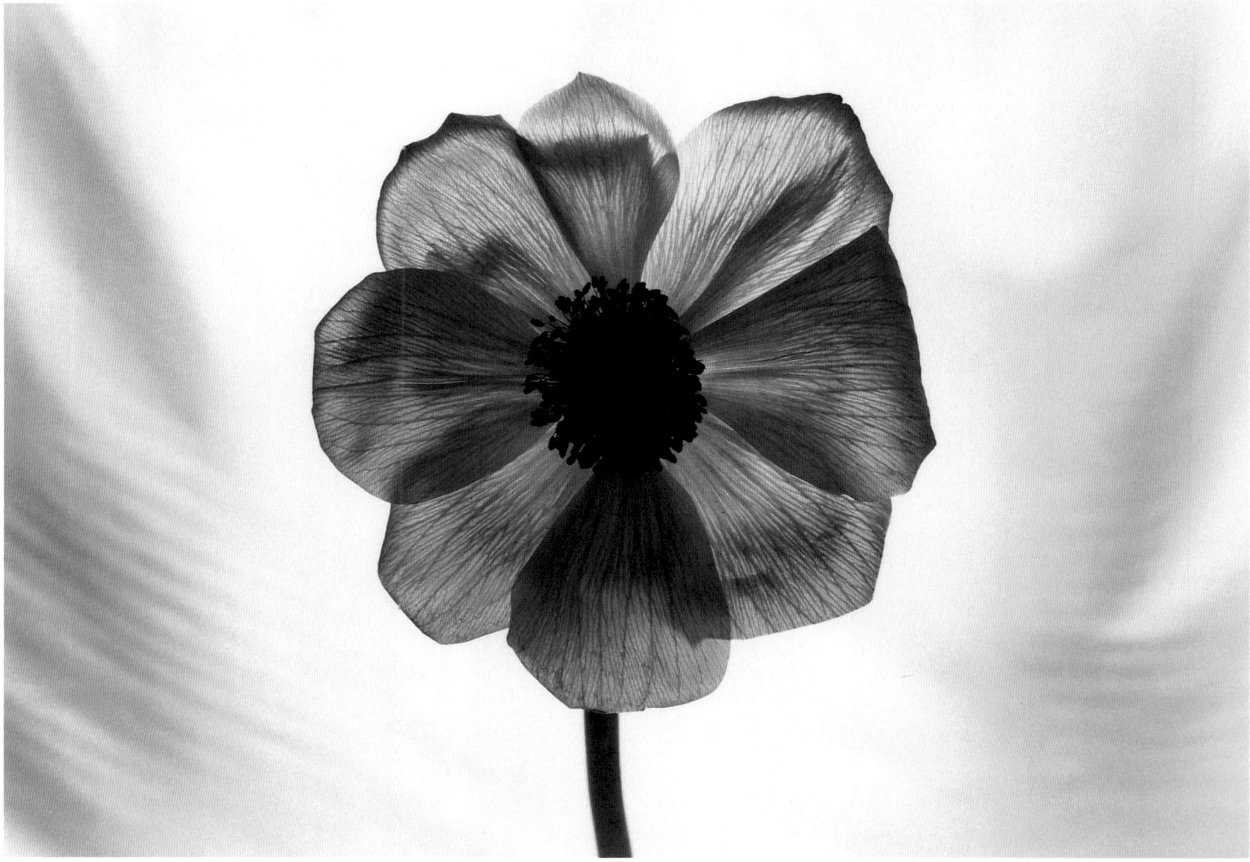

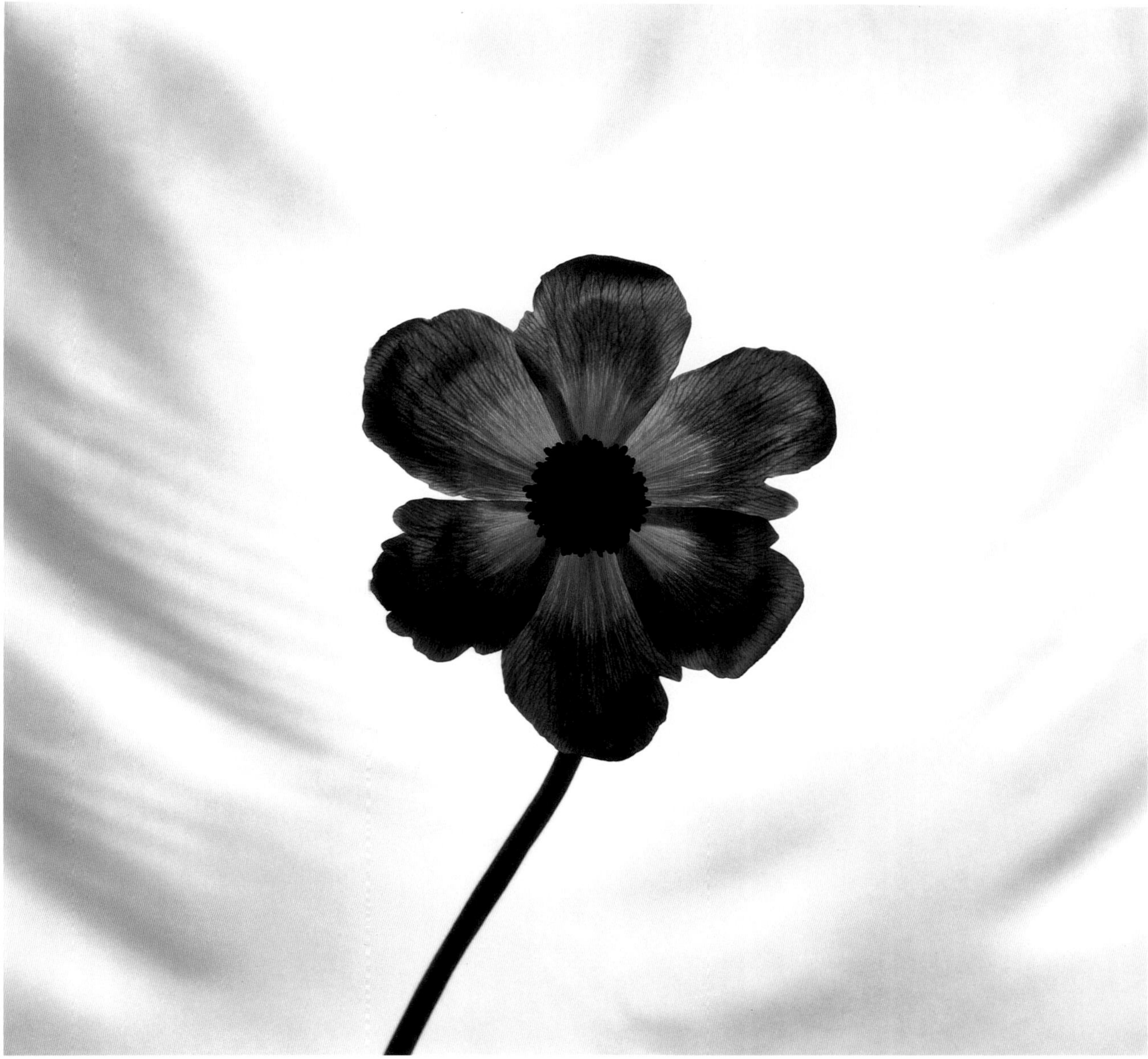

As the images took on a collective life, the connotations of "stance" expanded further. I began to realize that light values are not necessarily mere adjuncts of gesture, but can, of themselves, be gestural: the extreme tonal values of certain images connect them to one another, and to a deeper resonance as well.

The black anemones have depth and imply secrecy, yet their blackness is not opaque; it yields. The white flowers are of a tonal value that matches the satin; like voices in a fugue, figure and ground are distinct, yet part of the same substance. And, finally, there is a quality of tone that surpasses whiteness and approaches the feeling of glass. In these images, crystallinity itself is a metaphor: for what is translucency but nakedness to light?

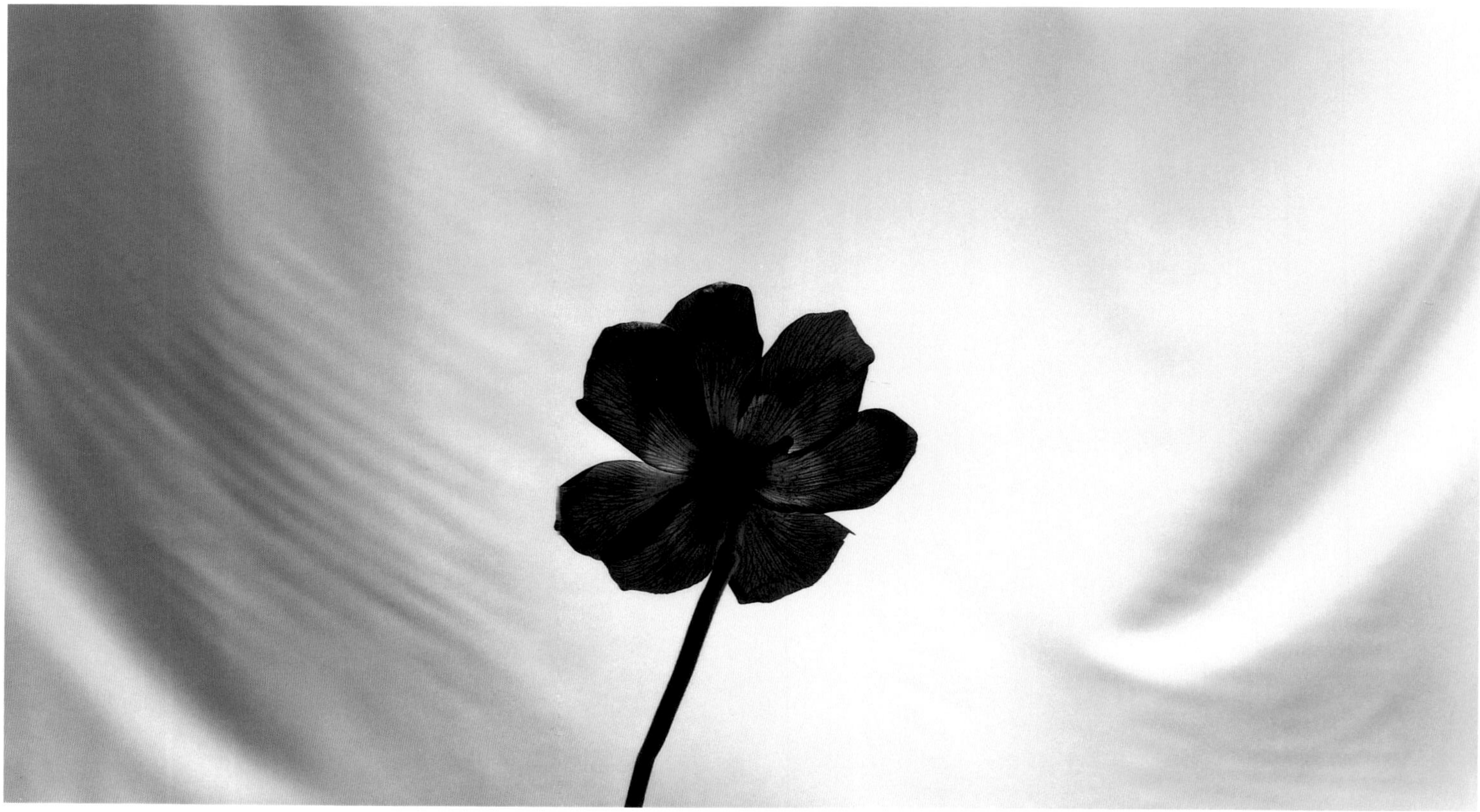

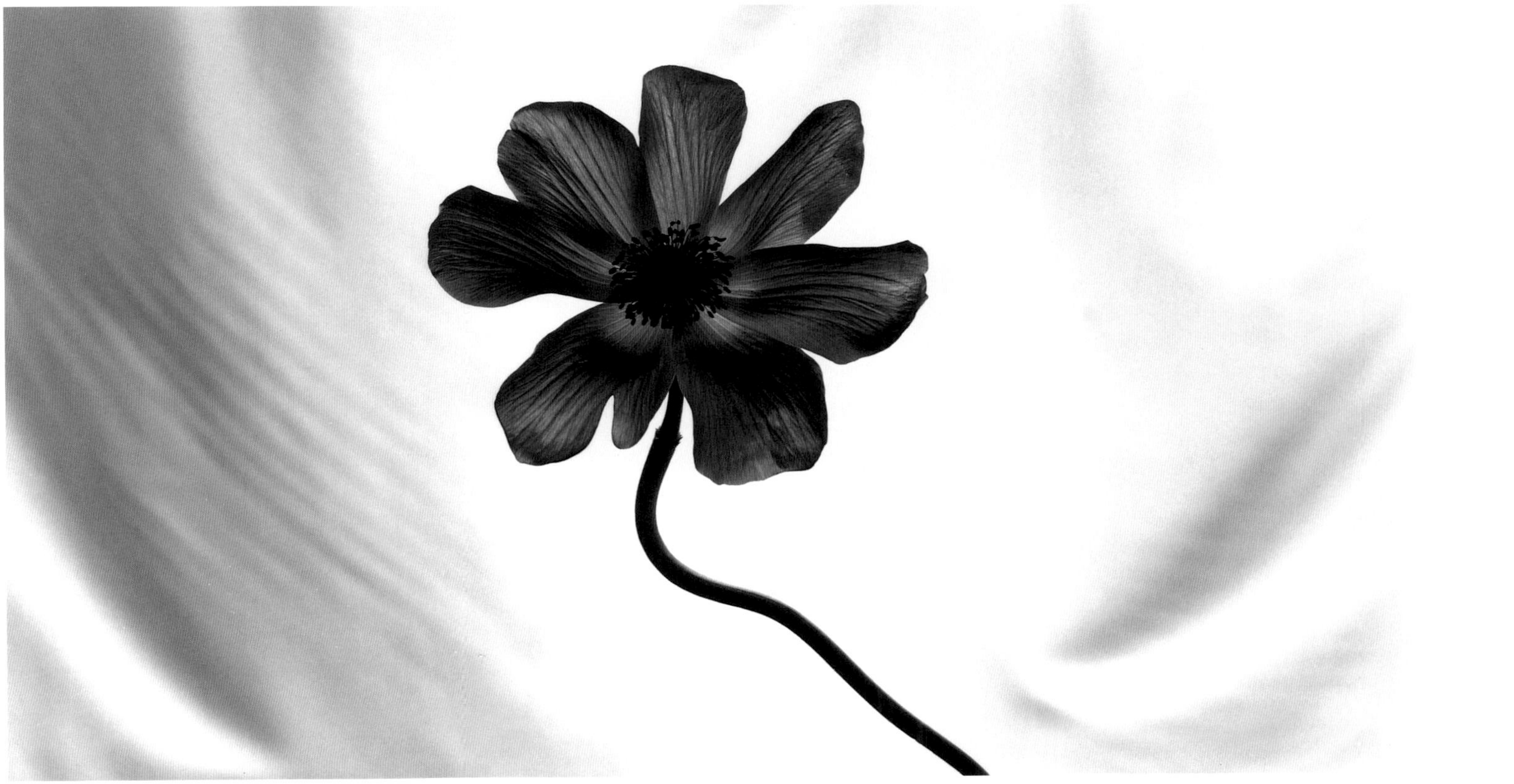

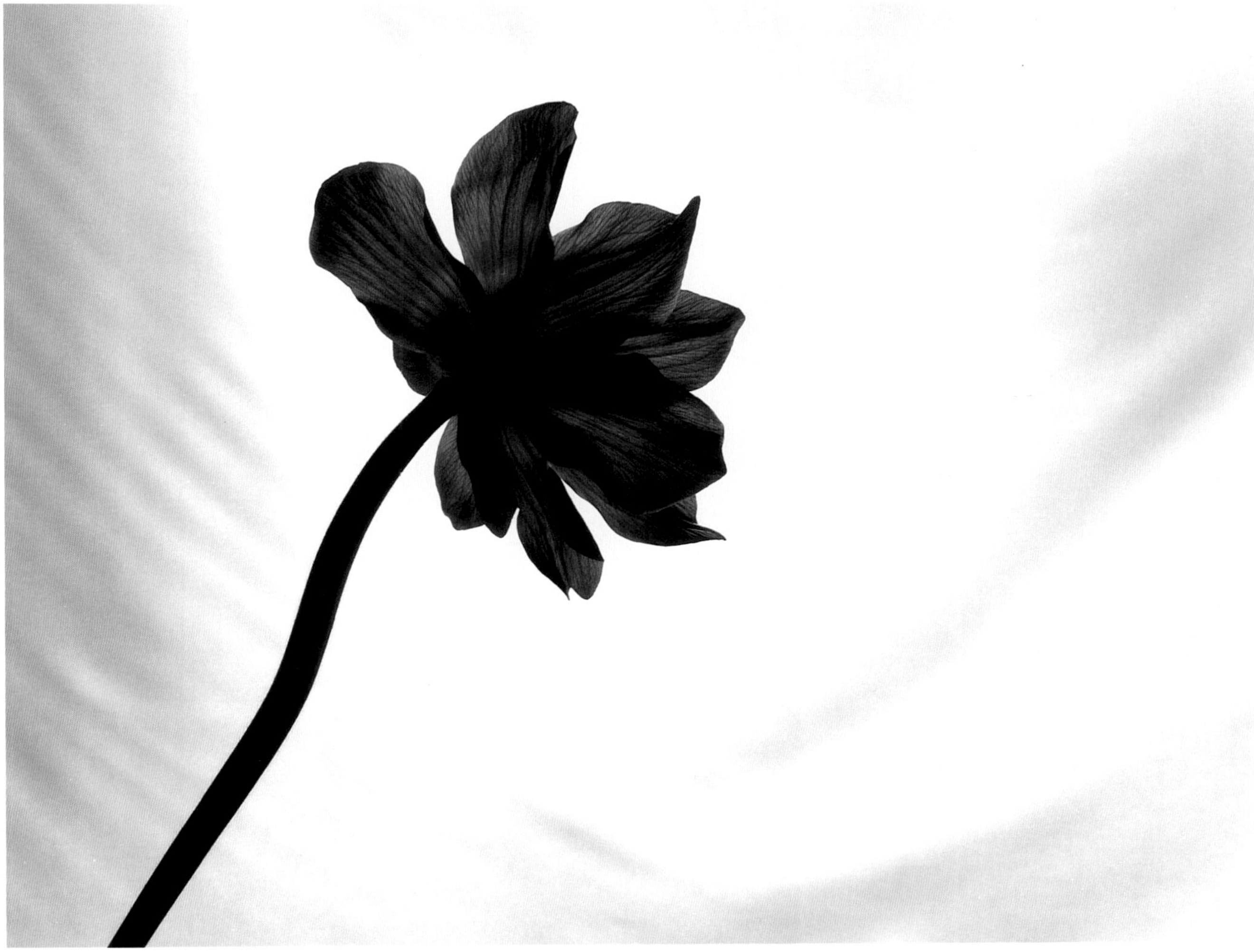

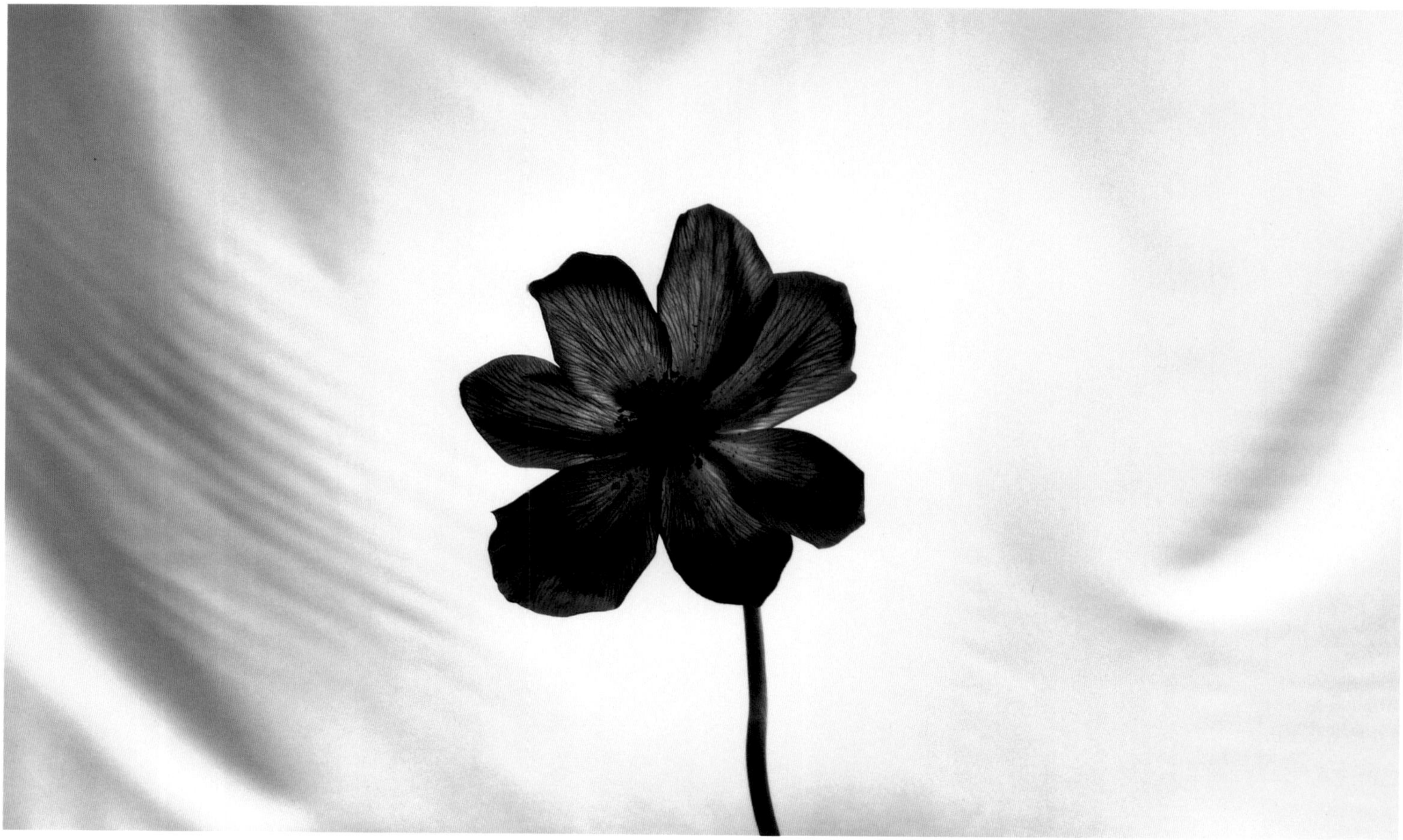

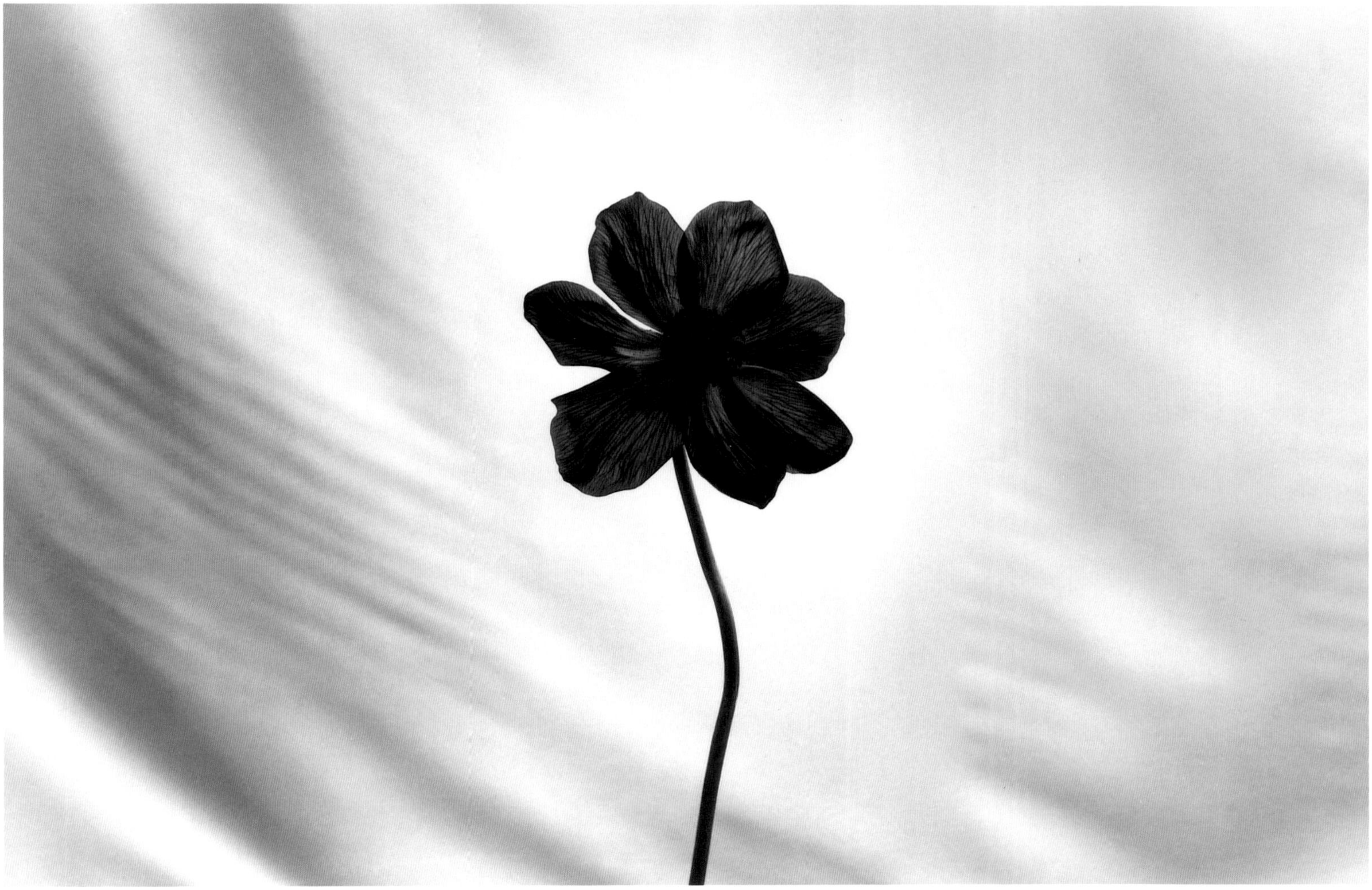

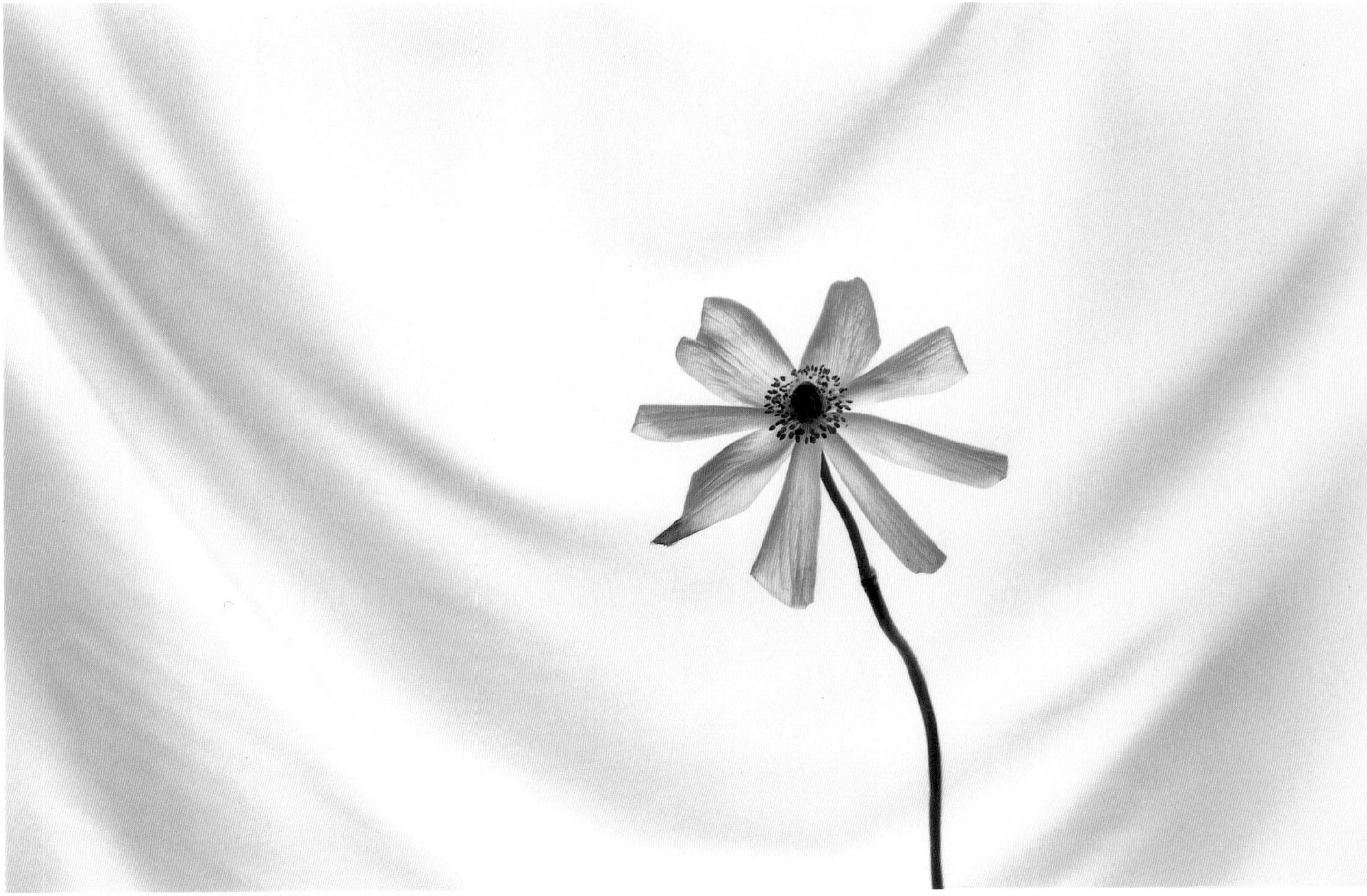

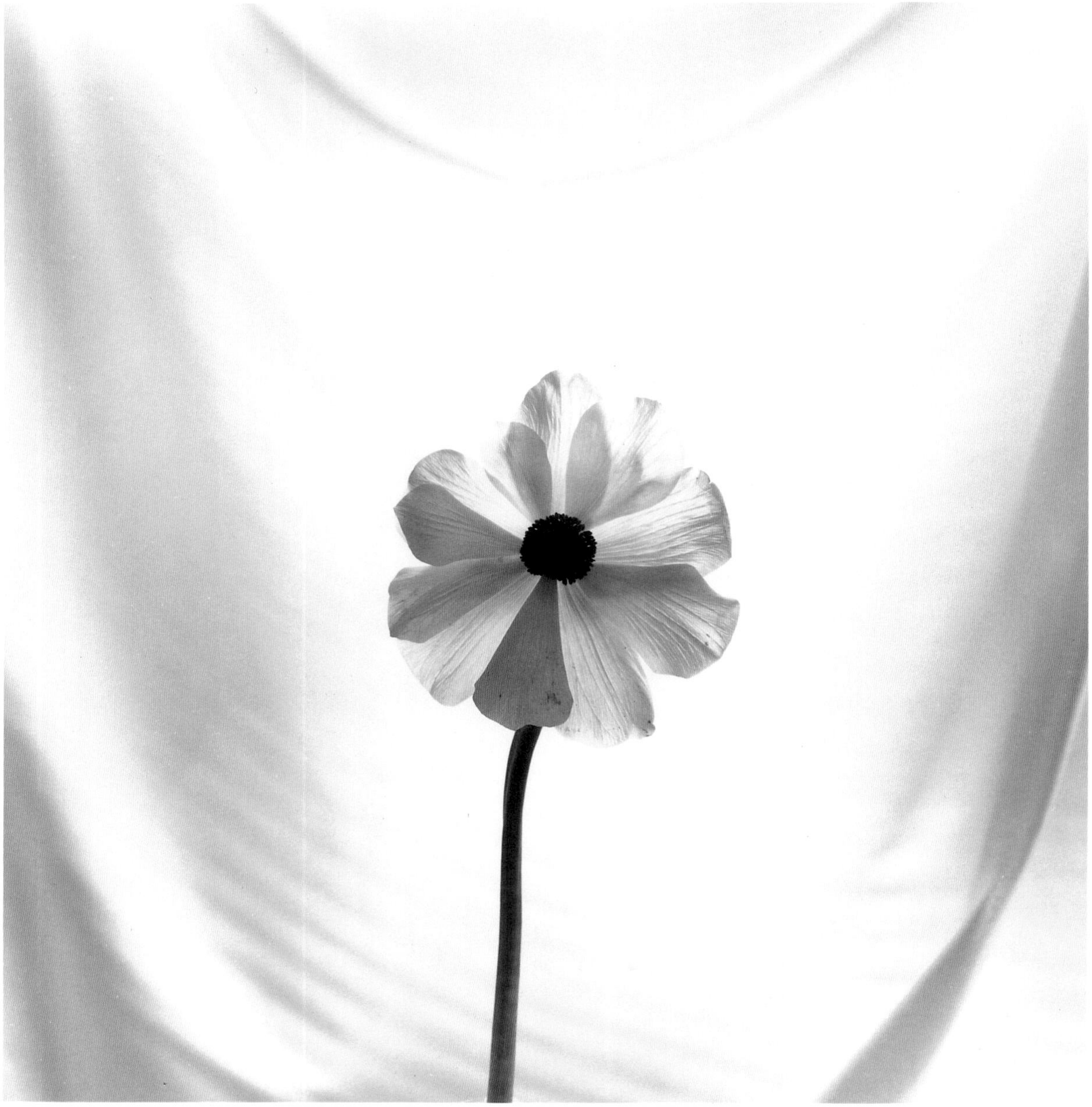

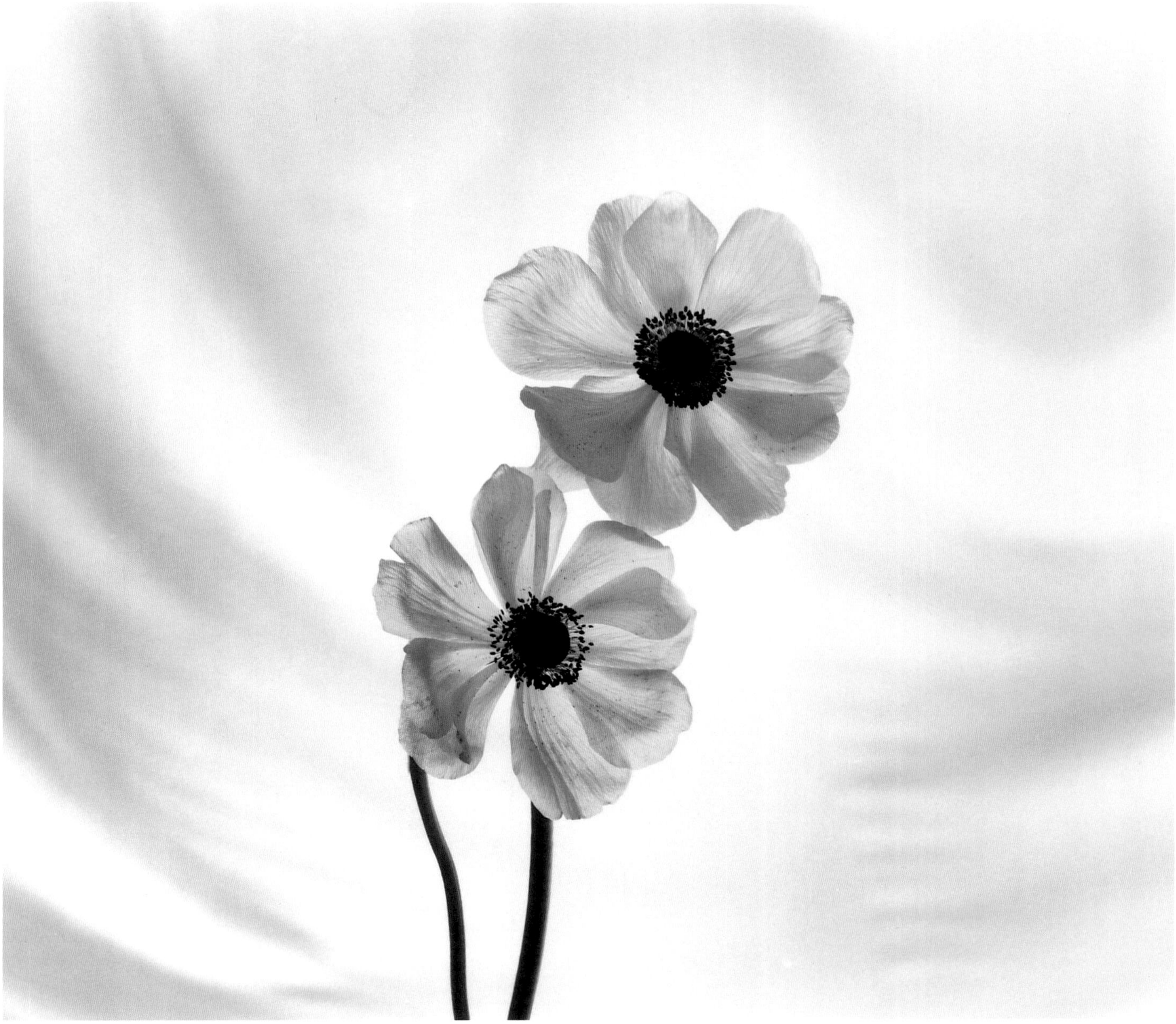

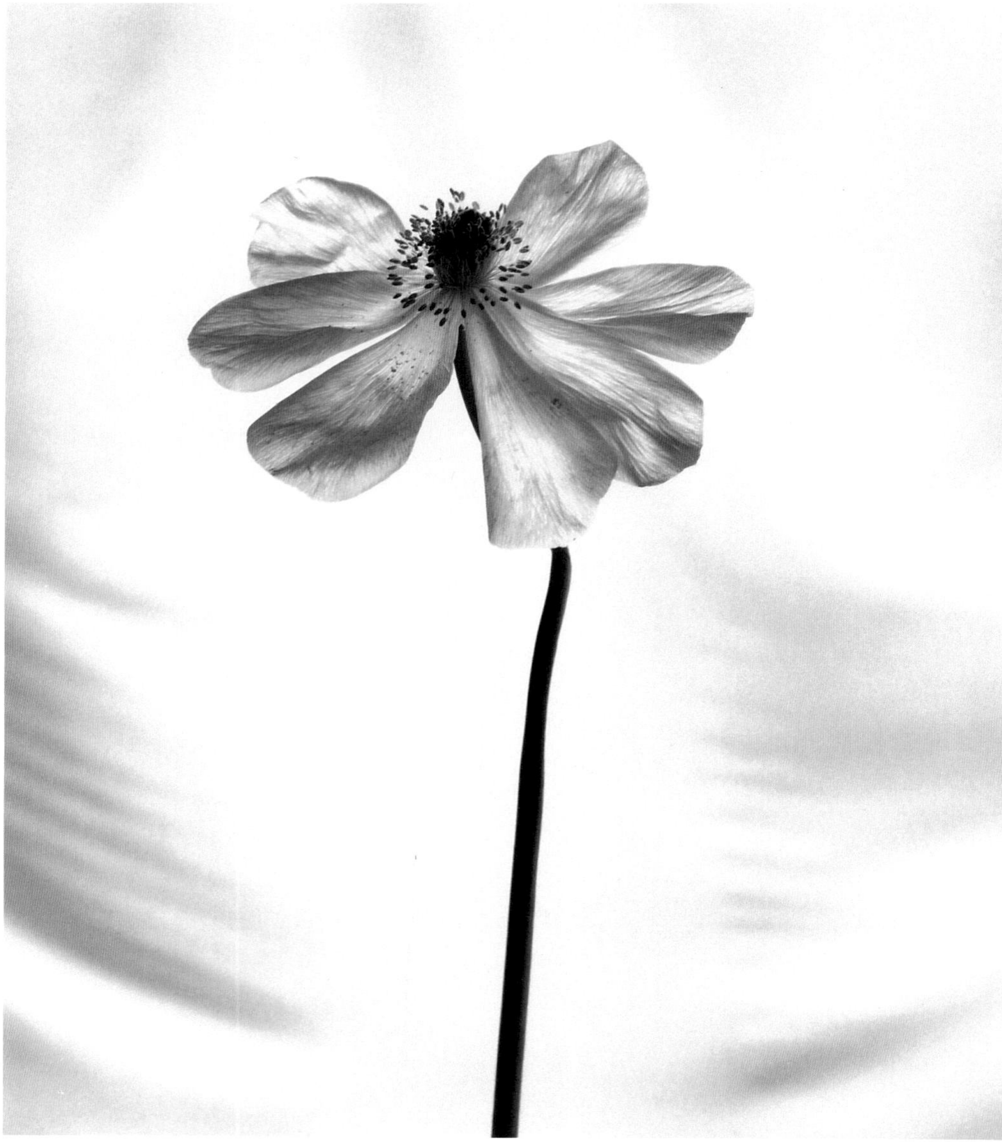

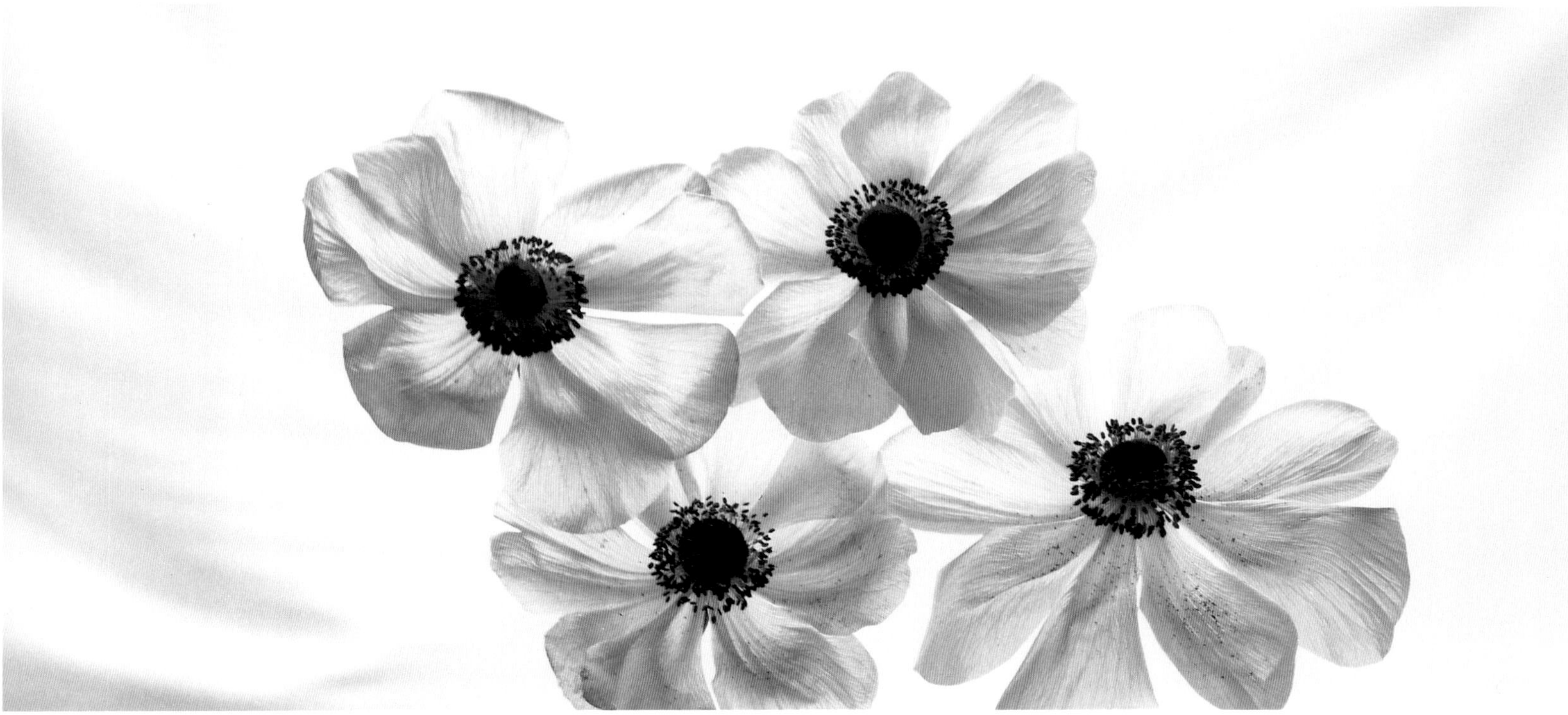

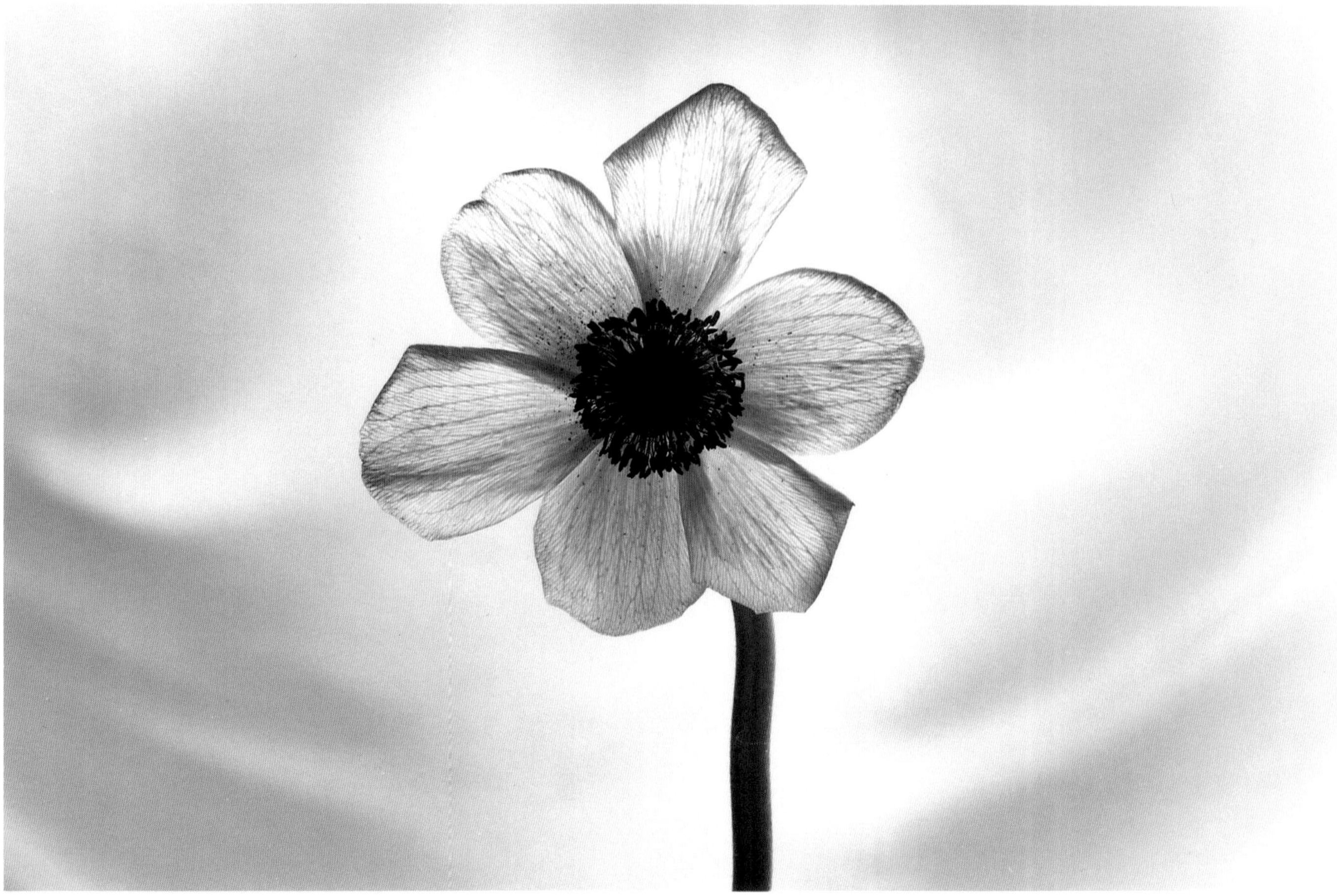

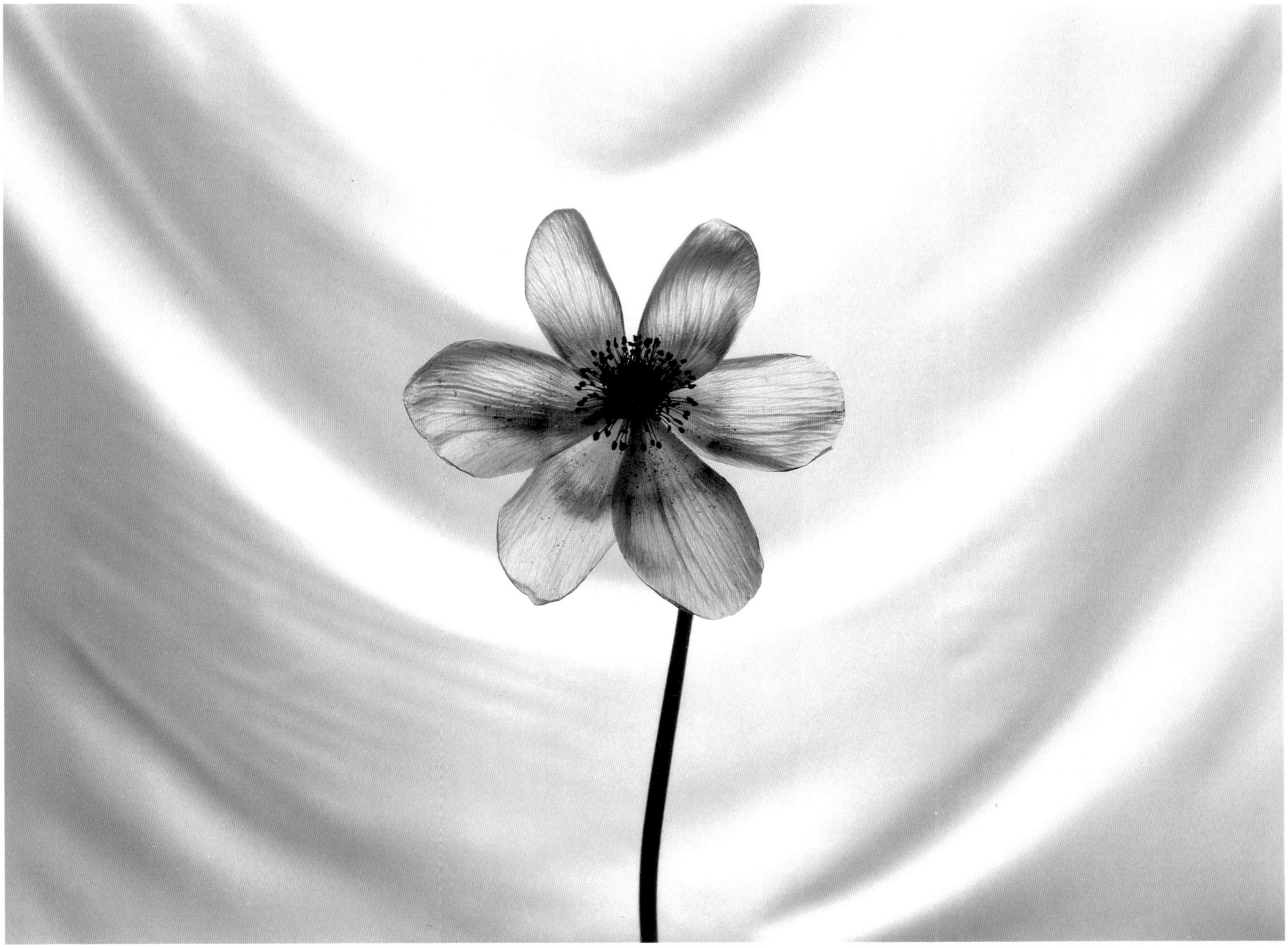

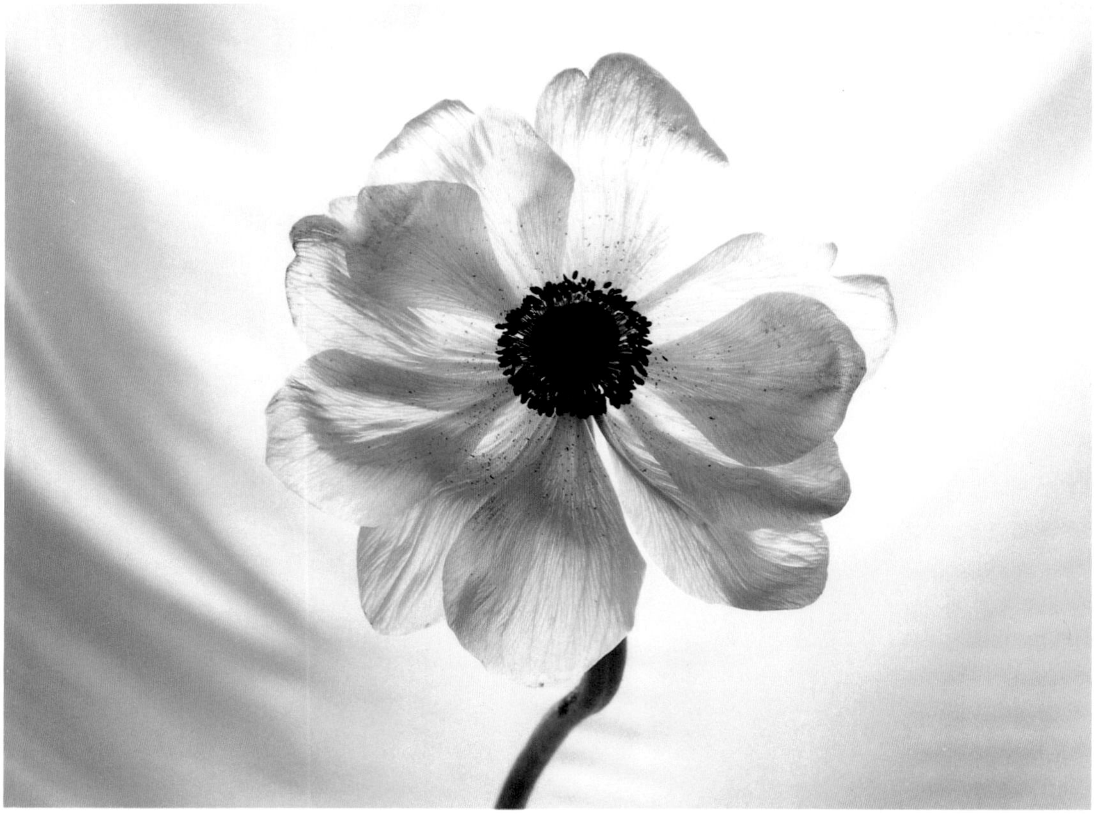

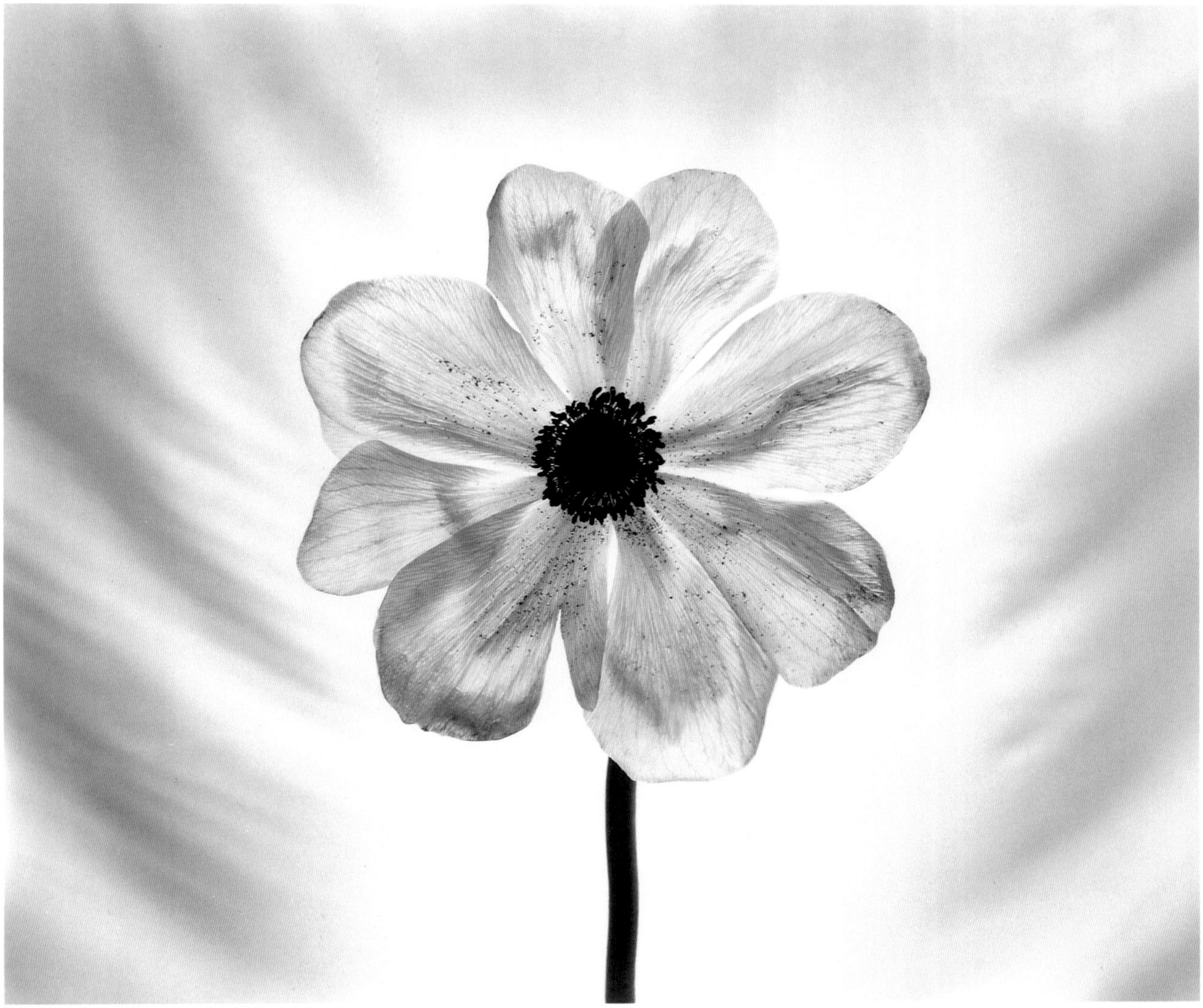

CAMERA OBSCURA: A MEDITATION

The question that dominates my life is why do I have to die. And how am I going to face it. In the Jewish religion, there is a ceremony that takes place a year after death called "the unveiling," a ceremony that takes place at the grave site where the headstone is "unveiled" or erected, and it is the family's final ritual of mourning, the last acceptance of the passing of the person's life. Because Jews believe that, despite an unknowable afterlife, human life must be lived as if complete in itself, and that real immortality comes to us through our descendants, as well as through the "monuments" to ourselves that we leave behind, such as our works, the idea of the unveiling has always intrigued me, as if it were a final revelation of why it should not be so fearful to die.

As I get older, there is no question that I need light more and more badly. The obvious metaphor of light as life is embedded in me, and as I fear progressively that final loss of light, I crave it more passionately in my daily existence. And I get more and more caught up in the art of photography, which is, of course, about light. My fascination for the desert, which has always been strong, grows as I perceive it as the place where light is never obscured; and my love of that desert city of lights, Las Vegas, becomes the entire subject for an epic poem of the West, where neon glitter adds to the sun's brilliance. The twenty-four hour city, and for me, by implication, the city where you never have to die.

Solving the problem of creating something that seems to last longer than it actually does—contrast this with the fact that a cosmic view of the universe makes one realize that events last only fractionally in comparison with even a light year, the time it takes light to travel a given distance—is every artist's task. Possibly, it is only when we are doing this that we can slightly forget the fear, if we have it (as I do, so badly) of why must we die. Lynn says that she started this project by trying to photograph light as it interacted with her scrim of thin satin cloth, but got caught up in the elegance of the material and its shapes. And it is true that in the first photographs, those of the draped cloth alone, one could entirely forget about light because of the beauty of the shapes, though one could argue that those shapes are shadows, which are aspects of the light she was photographing. Moving on to the task of photographing the flower, the anemone, she attempted an interesting experiment, working only with black and white, since the anemone is a flower one associates with color and brilliance. And, of course, color literally *is* light, different wave lengths creating different colors, and I suspect that it is during this meditation that I begin to think about how relevant this experiment in photography is to my own obsessive and terrifying concerns right now about dying, and to my trying to find metaphors or ways of understanding death so I can finally, if not understand it, accept it. What, I say, does it mean to try to understand light by divorcing it from some of its properties? For instance, if light equals life, and lack of light equals death, how far can you shut the process down and still have life? How much can you remove? Removing color, using only the white and the black, is a little like aging, taking the freshness out of something.

Even though it was certainly not the photographer's purpose to give me material for meditating on my own problems, she did make me wonder, as I looked at each different version of an anemone, that light is manifested in so many different ways that even the absence of light, at least in the form of the black anemone, is another form of it. This tantalizes me, though it offers no comfort or respite from my fear, and it leads me to another meditation: on the subject of memory. Memory is the residue of an event. But the longer memory is nourished, the more it becomes a re-creation of the event, perhaps even an invention of it (it is often so far from a document), so that not only is it residue, but it might be larger, more significant than the event that caused it. Memory is a kind of interior light. If the event is life, and life is light, then when the event ceases there should be no light. But the residue of the event, which becomes memory and which, if the memory is important, grows, may in fact become an interior light even brighter than the light of the actual event.

Looking at the black anemones and thinking about black as an absence of light, but knowing that those black anemones were studies of light and that photography is only light, I began to understand even more what an important part of life memory is. Aging, which has always seemed so awful to me, for obvious reasons, including the fact that it is the process of journeying towards death, has taken on a new meaning for me since I am able to think of it through my meditations on memory and light. Memory only exists because we age, i.e., have experiences that are now past. Is there a paradox then: that we only have this interior light as we are losing life/time, the exterior light? I am not sure, but the photography and problems of light, such as those Lynn Stern is trying to solve, seem right at the heart of metaphysics to me, and I am grateful to have them as objects for this meditation.

The following poem is one I wrote last year, and the "camera" in the title is meant to be a pun, in addition to the literal meaning of the term, on the word "camera," which means secret, death being, of course, the biggest secret of all.

CAMERA OBSCURA

DIANE WAKOSKI
EAST LANSING, 1987

For the light
that fills everything:

you need
a desert
or scrubby
non-forested land.

To be surrounded
by light,
to be permeated with
its radiance

to be part
of the dazzle
in the morning
when you wake from everynight's
curtained death,

when you need
no shadows,
want
nothing,
but pure
morning/desert/light,

when you need it,
but do not have it,
when memory
must be
everything.

The eye closes
its aperture;
Mind opens/uses
its slowest
shutter speed.

UNVEILINGS

was designed by Katy Homans,

produced by Nan Jernigan,

edited and copyedited by Terry Reece Hackford and Robin Jacobson, and

typeset by Trufont Typographers.

The laser-scanned duotones, printing, and binding are by Meriden-Stinehour Press.

The paper is Warren's Lustro Dull.